THE A–Z OF ADDRESSING DISADVANTAGE

MARC ROWLAND
SERIES EDITOR: ROY BLATCHFORD

Together we unlock every learner's unique potential

At Hachette Learning (formerly Hodder Education), there's one thing we're certain about. No two students learn the same way. That's why our approach to teaching begins by recognising the needs of individuals first.

Our mission is to allow every learner to fulfil their unique potential by empowering those who teach them. From our expert teaching and learning resources to our digital educational tools that make learning easier and more accessible for all, we provide solutions designed to maximise the impact of learning for every teacher, parent and student.

Aligned to our parent company, Hachette Livre, founded in 1826, we pride ourselves on being a learning solutions provider with a global footprint.

www.hachettelearning.com

Although every effort has been made to ensure that website addresses are correct at time of going to press, Hachette Learning cannot be held responsible for the content of any website mentioned in this book. It is sometimes possible to find a relocated web page by typing in the address of the home page for a website in the URL window of your browser.

Hachette UK's policy is to use papers that are natural, renewable and recyclable products and made from wood grown in well-managed forests and other controlled sources. The logging and manufacturing processes are expected to conform to the environmental regulations of the country of origin.

To order, please visit www.HachetteLearning.com or contact Customer Service at education@hachette.co.uk / +44 (0)1235 827827.

ISBN: 978 1 0360 0496 5

© Marc Rowland 2025

First published in 2025 by
Hachette Learning,
An Hachette UK Company
Carmelite House
50 Victoria Embankment
London EC4Y 0DZ
www.HachetteLearning.com

The authorised representative in the EEA is Hachette Ireland, 8 Castlecourt Centre, Dublin 15, D15 XTP3, Ireland (email: info@hbgi.ie)

Impression number   10 9 8 7 6 5 4 3 2 1
Year   2029 2028 2027 2026 2025

All rights reserved. Apart from any use permitted under UK copyright law, no part of this publication may be reproduced or transmitted in any form or by any means, electronic or mechanical, including photocopying and recording, or held within any information storage and retrieval system, without permission in writing from the publisher or under licence from the Copyright Licensing Agency Limited. Further details of such licences (for reprographic reproduction) may be obtained from the Copyright Licensing Agency Limited, www.cla.co.uk

Illustrations by DC Graphic Design Limited, Hextable, Kent
Typeset in the UK.
Printed in the UK by CPI Group (UK) Ltd, Croydon CR0 4YY.

A catalogue record for this title is available from the British Library.

CONTENTS

About the author v
Foreword by Roy Blatchford vii

Section One

Ambition 3
Bias 11
Communication 19
Data 29
Evaluation 35
Families 41
Grouping 49
Homeroom 55
Implementation 67
Job 71
Kindness 77
Learning 83
Models 91
Needs 99
Oracy 109
Presumption 113
Quibbles 119
Research 125
Strategy 129

Transition 139

Uniting 143

Viola 147

Words 153

X-factor 159

Yahoo 163

Zeitgeist 167

Section Two

1. Research School Network articles 183

2. Tools 199

Acknowledgements 224

References 225

ABOUT THE AUTHOR

Marc Rowland is the adviser for improving outcomes for disadvantaged learners for the Unity Schools Partnership, a large cross-phase Trust based in the East of England.

Over his career he has worked with numerous Local Authorities, Multi Academy Trusts, Research Schools, Teaching School Hubs, English hubs and groups of schools nationally on long term projects to support better outcomes for disadvantaged pupils. He has led many area based programmes, from Cumbria to Cornwall focused on the experiences of disadvantaged pupils in schools and classrooms nationally. He has also been working with the Jersey government for eight years on the introduction and implementation of a 'Jersey Pupil Premium'. This has seen a marked improvement in outcomes over time for disadvantaged pupils there.

Marc has advised the Department for Education on making the best of the Pupil Premium in schools. He has worked with over 1000 individual schools to support them with their strategies to improve outcomes for disadvantaged pupils. Marc is the education adviser to the Driftwood Association, a Swiss charitable foundation running education and development projects in Nepal.

He has written extensively about improving educational outcomes for disadvantaged pupils, most recently with 'Transforming Attendance in Cornwall'. Marc's most recent book, 'Addressing Educational Disadvantage', was published in February 2021. The second edition of his award-winning book, 'An Updated Practical Guide to the Pupil Premium', was published in December 2015 (John Catt Educational). His book 'Learning without Labels' was published by John Catt in March 2017.

NOTE FROM THE AUTHOR

In this book, I have used the term 'disadvantage' in relation to pupils who grow up in low-income families. I know not everyone is comfortable with this, and want to acknowledge that. I recognise that this is an important debate.

For consistency, I have used the term in line with the language used by the Department for Education (DfE) in England. I want this resource to be practical and useful for schools.

The term 'pupil premium' has been used throughout this book. For those unfamiliar with this term, this is funding allocated to schools to improve educational outcomes for those pupils from disadvantaged backgrounds in the state school system. More information can be found at www.gov.uk/government/publications/pupil-premium.

I hope this book provokes some thinking. The attainment of disadvantaged pupils will not improve on its own. It won't improve by disappointment at the data. It will improve through reductions in child poverty. It will also improve by understanding the impact of low family income better, and how to respond to it in the classroom and wider school life. It will improve as we improve as an education system - from policy to the classroom and playground.

Marc Rowland

FOREWORD

It's the stuff of popular magazines. Interview a famous person about their childhood influences, their treasured moments and possessions, their faith, their biggest extravagance, who and what they find most irritating.

In a recent such interview, a Formula 1 racing driver, when asked what his childhood ambition was, replied: 'To be a farmer – I thought tractors were just brilliant. Then greenkeeper at a golf course, because of all the different lawnmowers. Then I realised you could go a lot faster.'

Another interviewee, a distinguished mathematician, answered: 'To be a professional 10-pin bowler. Then an astronaut.' And a third admitted: 'To make friends with a wolf.'

There is a particular question often asked of interviewees that invariably elicits thoughtful responses: 'Which matters more to success: ambition or talent?' One person will observe that both are ingredients to success but that luck is even more important. Another will suggest that passion makes the chances of success greater. A number of key words are often used in answers to this question: opportunity, confidence, inner gift, discipline.

As a teacher, I used to display in my classroom this extract from Miroslav Holub's poem *A Boy's Head* (2006) at the start of every academic year.

> In it there is a space-ship
> and a project
> for doing away with piano lessons.
>
> There is a river
> that flows upwards.
>
> There is a multiplication table.
>
> There is anti-matter. And it just cannot be trimmed.

I believe
that only what cannot be trimmed
is a head.

There is much promise
In the circumstance
That so many people have heads.

The poem served as a constant reminder of the endless possibilities that rest inside the minds of the pupils – and that it is every teacher's challenge to unlock those possibilities.

The highly respected Education Policy Institute's annual reports (2024) offer sober scrutiny of the gaps that exist between disadvantaged pupils and their peers. The analyses by geographical region, ethnicity and GCSE subject make for arresting reading and should be the focus of discussion in every staffroom across the country.

So, what can we do in our own classrooms to realise the ambitions and talents of those who look to us for guidance and inspiration? Let us take every opportunity to spot the inner gift of a pupil. Let us nurture confidence in the shy student. Let us help young people to believe in their abilities and develop a latent talent. How a young person feels about themselves – their personal dignity and self-esteem – lies at the heart of a good education.

The teacher's optimistic, long-established trade is one of talent spotting and helping students to realise their ambitions; enabling all young people to attain well and achieve with pride. There is always much promise in our classrooms.

And it is that underpinning optimism that characterises *The A–Z of Addressing Disadvantage*. Section One is ordered around the 26 letters of the English alphabet. Section Two is a veritable mine of practical materials.

The author's belief in every child realising their social and academic potential shines on every page. He has visited many thousands of classrooms – north, south, east, west – as an ambassador for underserved, vulnerable children and young people. His experiences in those classrooms are writ large in this book.

Marc Rowland takes us from **Bias** and **Data** through **Homeroom** and **Kindness** to **Quibbles** and **Viola**: a sequence of authoritative and highly readable chapters, packed full of examples, ideas and reflections. His relentless focus is upon how staff in primary, special and secondary schools can best address disadvantage – with clarity, sensitivity and impact.

Roy Blatchford, series editor

SECTION ONE

AMBITION

The attainment gap found in UK schools reflects the broader inequalities in society. Low family income and low attainment are still too closely linked. This book looks to support school leaders at all levels to plan, implement and evaluate an effective disadvantage strategy. It aims to support schools and system leaders to enable pupils to thrive, irrespective of background and starting point. Ambition matters.

The book does not look to replicate guidance on teaching and learning or school leadership. These are covered in other titles in the A–Z series and elsewhere. It will also not replicate or recreate other resources such as guidance from the Education Endowment Foundation (EEF). Rather, it will guide school leaders and system leaders based on nearly a decade and a half of work solely focused on trying to understand what is happening in schools and classrooms where pupils from low-income backgrounds are thriving, and in schools that are finding this stubborn issue a tougher nut to crack.

It draws on the inspirational work of teachers, leaders and support staff from across the UK. It aims to provoke thinking and reflection to support those 'at the chalk face' of school leadership and in the classroom.

Reports about the disadvantage gap are published annually. These may be followed by commentators making statements in the media and on social media declaring that 'something should be done', but it is often the case that little follows.

Efforts to address socioeconomic disadvantage in society and provide support for disadvantaged pupils in our education system have lacked political leadership for some time, since David Laws finished being Schools Minister in 2015.

Furthermore, the lack of focus on disadvantaged pupils in the current (2019) Ofsted framework has been a disaster. Schools *have* to be responsive to the framework. We need clarity and focus from policy to the classroom. The proposals for 2025 onwards have a far stronger focus on disadvantage, giving this far greater prominence. We can do better in schools, particularly if we have more clarity over what schools should be doing, and what schools should *not* be doing, to support disadvantaged pupils. We need to be more boundaried, and not lose sight of what is happening in our classrooms for disadvantaged pupils every day. Should it be the role of teachers, particularly those that are inexperienced, to be picking vulnerable pupils up and bringing them into school? This puts pressure on teachers and can impact on the classroom, staff wellbeing, etc.

Disadvantaged pupils thrive when teachers *enjoy* teaching. There is something about teaching and learning that cannot actually be codified; that connection between pupil(s) and teacher, rooted in a trusting relationship, where pupils feel that the teacher is sat alongside them and is their *champion*. There is no single way to model this, to explain it, to exemplify it. It is something individual to the teacher and the pupils in the classroom.

It is about the teacher's ability to be responsive to the individuals in their classroom and in wider school life – in formal instruction and informal conversation. This relationship is important for all pupils, but is particularly important for those that experience the insecurity of low family income and the cold wind of poverty. Susie Fraser from Manchester Communication Academy (MCA) exemplifies it here.

> *I guess the way that we approach this at MCA ... it's a core value. We believe that all students can be anything that they can achieve. And despite them being disadvantaged, they are individual students with amazing talents and amazing possibilities.*
>
> *It's our job really to find the best way to empower our pupils. One thing I have learned from working at MCA is that we don't need to lower expectations, or do things differently. We want students that are resilient and have grit. Our students have that in abundance. Their circumstances mean that even just to walk through the door at school in the morning shows strength of character and resilience.*

There is so much joy and love and support and talent within our community. It is our job to find out how we can fit in to that community and contribute.

When we recruit, we recruit on values. I think – for the most part – you can train people to be a better teacher. You can refine their expertise, but you can't really teach values. So that's a big part of our recruitment process. It is really important to us. We want to create a culture of wellbeing, so staff give their all, give their best to our students. Happy teachers means happy students. Wellbeing is about investing in staff – in their professional development – so they know how they're being asked to act and interact, rather than try lots of different things. Our work is based on research evidence. We make that a real priority.

Our approach is to build a team that has genuine and authentic relationships with families. Not just with the students, but you get to know siblings ... and think about how we might be able to support it if there are any difficulties around health or finance or housing. We have a team that have been trained to know where to signpost, give advice and support families, and serve the community. We build that relationship with the family, so they know that they can trust the school. This means students are more likely to attend. It is an investment. It's about values, beliefs and our aspirations. We do not allow a deficit narrative. We know that we can make a difference.

We need urgency in improving the consistency of understanding and levels of expertise in schools around addressing disadvantage, from strategy to the classroom. Building this expertise is still too 'optional' and variable'.

The attainment of disadvantaged pupils is still not improving sufficiently across all schools and settings. Having a clear, robust strategy around this is vital.

As I write, there is no clarity and consistency over national policy for addressing educational disadvantage. We need to create this locally, in our schools and communities. This should include a consistent message about what is and what is not the remit of schools.

WHAT IS HAPPENING IN SCHOOLS WHERE DISADVANTAGED PUPILS ARE THRIVING?

I have had the privilege of visiting and working with leaders, teachers and pupils in schools where pupils facing disadvantage are thriving. The following themes seem to stand out:

- Commit to the principle that working with disadvantaged pupils is a privilege, not a problem to resolve.
- Coalesce a culture and belief that all pupils, irrespective of background or starting point, can attain well and thrive in wider school life.
- Understand low family income and its impact on opportunity, child development and health. Understand the impact of low family income on children inside school and out.
- Agree, as a school, that low family income should never be a barrier to opportunity in the classroom and wider school life. Family income should never be an obstacle to accessing all that school has to offer. Curriculum trips should never be inaccessible for those whose families cannot (or do not want to) pay. The impact is not just lost academic learning, but social exclusion.
- Never lower expectations based on a family's ability or capacity to support learning. Family capacity to support a child's education should not impact on our ambitions for pupils. If a parent is struggling to support the literacy development of a child at home (for lots of complex reasons), that pupil needs time, expertise and support in school.
- Pupils cannot be held accountable for parental decisions, and low family income may well mean that some families are just trying to get through every day, rather than thinking long term. (It is important that there is colour and joy within difficult lives. Joyful moments should not be the preserve of the better off.)
- Labels should not determine activity. Adopt a more nuanced, learning-led approach. We should focus activity on the learning needs of pupils, rather than their Pupil Premium (PP) eligibility (or otherwise). This puts the ownership on the teacher. Furthermore, it avoids inadvertently isolating pupils, and there are lots of pupils in

our education system growing up in low-income families that are not eligible for the PP. Nuance is key. Teacher agency is key.

FOCUS ON THE LEARNER, NOT THE LABEL

The models below set out how we can focus on the learner, rather than more performative, label-led approaches:

By focusing on pupils as individuals, we:	Overly focusing on labels such as PP means we:
• empower teachers • socially include pupils • promote teacher agency • are driven by needs first • intervene to address underlying causes.	• anonymise pupils • create social isolation • try to intervene to labels or symptoms • remove teacher agency • prioritise compliance.

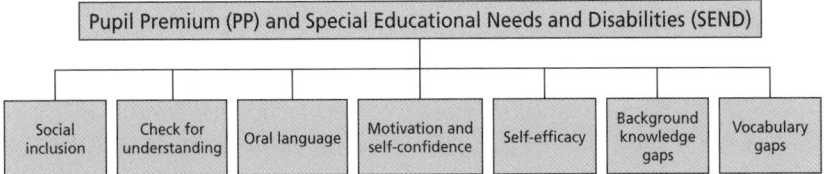

The importance of focusing on the learner, rather than the label

- Labels should not be used as a reason for underachievement. Pupils are not at risk of underachievement because they are 'Pupil Premium' or 'SEND' (special educational needs and disabilities). Dig deeper. These labels say very little about pupils. We cannot intervene to a label or an umbrella term. Furthermore, the PP and SEND labels can lead to staff being overwhelmed and disempowered. Understand the *need*.

- Assessment, not assumption, should always be at the heart of every strategy. Providing meaningful, actionable data to teachers and curriculum/pastoral leaders is key.

- Recognise that pupils are largely consistent in their behaviours, actions and attitudes (even when their actions aren't quite in line with our expectations!). All too often, we, the adults, are the variable. This might be in relation to strategic issues such as staff recruitment and staff wellbeing. It may be more day-to-day issues such as staff attendance, behaviour management, relationships and formative assessment. The most effective strategies give staff the capacity, expertise, knowledge and support to help pupils to thrive.

- If I don't ensure that pupils take down a worked example in their books, but my co-teacher always checks and ensures that pupils have done so, I am the variable when I need to be the consistent. If I don't ensure that all pupils are participating in echo reading, but my co-teacher does, I am the variable. If I am not checking pupils' responses in my phonics session, or if I allow opt out but my colleagues do not, I am the variable. If I am not economic with my explanations, if I talk during the silent 'do now' task, or if I don't use the agreed signal for silence, I am the variable. This disproportionately impacts on pupils that need consistency and clarity in their lives.
- Disadvantaged pupils are rarely confident enough to manage sarcasm. As Kay Turner from Sigma Trust says: 'we need to be much more mindful in our interactions with students for whom school is hard enough and/or those whose confidence in the nuances of language is more fragile. For some children these throwaway comments take on a significance that most teachers cannot begin to imagine.'
- The purpose of childhood is to be a child: to push boundaries, to try things out, to take on risk and challenge. This can look different at different phases of childhood. Pupils want to feel like they are successful and that they belong. If they are not being successful academically, or in wider school life, they will find other ways to belong.
- Focus on high-leverage issues that benefit and support all learners: self-regulation, oral language, background knowledge and reading. If we are to improve pupils as learners and help them to thrive, most roads lead back to reading. See lesson planning and enactment through the lens of disadvantaged pupils.
- Use tutoring and intervention to supplement, not supplant, high-quality teaching. Successful interventions should see gains sustained back in the classroom.
- Don't ignore personal development as a key strand of an effective strategy. High-quality careers opportunities are often not available to

pupils from lower-income backgrounds. See this recent report from Speakers for Schools published in the *TES*: www.tes.com/magazine/news/secondary/half-state-school-students-disadvantaged-by-lack-of-work-experience-university-access.

- Ensure any focus on attendance is rooted in the drivers of poor attendance, not the symptoms. (Watch this video for more on this idea: https://vimeo.com/900841929/6e529b5e30.) Recognise that relationships are a key driver of social development.
- Recognise that any work with families should be targeted, clearly defined, achievable and rooted in a strength-based discourse. Recognise that the evidence about effective parental involvement changes depending on the ages of pupils.
- Dispassionate impact evaluation is key to better outcomes for pupils. We are not trying to prove we are successful – we are trying to understand whether what we are doing is working.

ASIDE

We don't address educational disadvantage through interventions. These have their place, but are only as effective as the universal provision. The better the universal provision, the more effective the interventions become. It takes a thousand little interactions – rooted in knowledge, understanding, care and expertise – to help disadvantaged pupils thrive. Over-intervention means that such pupils are socially isolated, and get a narrower experience than their peers. If we are not careful, pupils who get the broadest, richest experiences outside of school get the broadest, richest experiences in school. Academically, and in terms of personal development, this is the 'Matthew effect' in action.

Teachers and support staff matter. It is a huge privilege to be involved in this work. We have a unique opportunity to significantly help to shape the trajectory of the lives of young people. Not so that they can escape their communities, but to improve them. The experiences of disadvantaged pupils are transformed when they are perceived to be (and they perceive themselves to be) positive contributors to the school community.

BIAS

Bias exists in our education system, our schools and our classrooms. In the book *Thinking, Fast and Slow*, Daniel Kahneman (2011) has evidenced that people exhibit bias in their professional lives, often without being conscious of it. During interactions with particular pupils from particular backgrounds – or indeed, in interactions with labels such as 'low ability', 'Pupil Premium' and 'Pupil Premium and SEND' – our biases can emerge. Our biases can also emerge where teachers have positive perceptions of parenting, as evidenced in the University of Missouri study (2017):

> It's clear from years of research that teacher perceptions, even perceptions of which they are not aware, can greatly impact student success.... If a teacher has a good relationship with a student's parents or perceives that those parents are positively engaged in their child's education, that teacher may be more likely to give extra attention or go the extra mile for that student. If the same teacher perceives another child's parents to be uninvolved or to have a negative influence on the child's education, it likely will affect how the teacher interacts with both the child and the parent.

CONTROLLING FOR BIAS

The key to controlling for bias is to be open about it. The greatest risk around bias is to deny that it exists. Possible biases that might be problematic for disadvantaged pupils, without us being conscious of them, might include:

- attainment/ability labels: 'He is low ability.'

- categorisation labels: 'She is SEND/FSM (free school meals)/ Pupil Premium.'
- ethnicity: 'She is White British.'/'They have a real tiger mum.'
- gender: 'Girls and maths'
- class: 'They are working class.'
- multiple: 'He is a White British, working-class boy with SEND.'/'White British boys don't like reading.'
- family: 'His older brother really struggled.'/'They never read at home.'/'They never attend parents' evenings.'
- confidence: 'They never put their hand up in class.'/'They lack motivation.'
- subject-specific: 'He enjoys creative subjects.'

It is human to have biases, borne out of our experiences. But generalisations and biases can set limits on what pupils can achieve. It is why strategies to address disadvantage should be everyone's responsibility – so we can hold ourselves to account.

Note that bias around accents is still a significant barrier to social mobility, as set out in a report by the Sutton Trust (2022).

The most effective strategies focus on giving teachers and wider staff the capacity, expertise and development to meet the needs of their learners. To improve them as learners and help them to thrive in wider school life, teacher and wider staff agency buy-in are fundamental to success. Avoid performative approaches, rooted in compliance, such as 'PP first', that negate teacher expertise.

Developing culture is a continuous process, not an event. It should not be thought of as something 'to be achieved'. A shared language around efforts for supporting disadvantaged pupils is vital. From governance in the classroom to external support, staff should speak with one voice. Belief in learners matters.

Schools that are outward facing, engaging with and being challenged by research evidence, are places where disadvantaged pupils thrive. However, schools should also be inward facing. Pupils should be listened to – about their sense of inclusion in school life. Pupil voice may well surprise us. In our work, students consistently tell us that their teacher is more important than their subject, and that the most frustrating thing about school is a superficial check of understanding, not the state of the toilets (though they matter too!).

Recruitment and retention of high-quality staff, with expertise in the challenges faced by pupils, is key. Learners need maximum opportunities to work with high-quality, committed and stable staff.

Schools and staff should have the highest expectations of all learners and families. They should understand and be empathetic to those who, for any number of reasons, may find it more difficult to engage with school life.

For multiple, complex reasons, some pupils may find learning more difficult. Be mindful of not lowering expectations and aspirations for these learners. Nurture and support all learners to take pride in their individual achievements. Learners' contributions to lessons and wider school life should be encouraged and valued.

Priorities for disadvantaged learners should not be separated from school-wide priorities. Be proactive – unite as a school community focused on addressing disadvantage. Build a sense of inclusion and belonging for all.

Pupils lacking opportunities outside of school should play an active, full role in school life in the same way as those that are opportunity-rich outside of school. They should be expected to make the necessary progress to attain well. We should be restless about the attainment of pupils who lack a confident voice of support at home.

We need to be champions of our disadvantaged pupils. And we should never lower expectations or limit opportunity on account of family circumstances. Some families, for complex, or multiple reasons, might struggle to support their child's academic learning outside of school. No judgement is needed. Such pupils need championing and support.

Parental behaviours can exacerbate biases and align with our preconceived ideas. I used to fill out the reading records of my own children positively, irrespective of whether they had read or not, to help maintain positive perceptions from their teachers. (Don't judge me!)

'COACHED FOR THE CLASSROOM'

Full article available at: https://journals.sagepub.com/doi/10.1177/0003122414546931

ABSTRACT

Scholars typically view class socialisation as an implicit process. This study instead shows how parents actively transmit class-based cultures to children and how these lessons reproduce inequalities. Through observations and interviews with children, parents and teachers, I found that middle- and working-class parents expressed contrasting beliefs about appropriate classroom behaviour – beliefs that shaped parents' cultural coaching efforts. These efforts led children to activate class-based problem-solving strategies, which generated stratified profits at school. By showing how these processes vary along social class lines, this study reveals a key source of children's class-based behaviours and highlights the efforts by which parents and children together reproduce inequalities.

WORKING WITH FAMILIES

Questions to consider:

- What constitutes effective parental engagement?
- How should we evaluate it?
- How can we improve what we do around working with parents?
- What types of parental involvement do we not like (be honest!)?

Practicalities

- There are very few parental involvement programmes or interventions that have a causal impact on pupil attainment.
- We know it's important but know little about how to influence it.
- We can't be successful with parental involvement if we don't define it.
- Parental involvement improves when children are successful socially and academically.

- Working to develop positive attitudes and dispositions matters most. Families need to feel part of the school community.
- Video may be far more effective at reaching all families than a traditional newsletter.
- A collective responsibility is key (school reception to the classroom!).
- Remembering that agency, power and confidence hugely influence bahaviours.

How a middle class 'by any means' approach results in learning gains (with thanks to Cathy Potter)

Middle class 'By any means'	Working class 'No excuses'
Parents intervene to get accommodations, assessments, support	Parents try to manage how their family is perceived by others
Feel their own assessment of child's ability & needs is equal/superior to teacher	Parents expect communicating with school/requests will result in negative perception of the family
Parents expect communicating with school/requests will result in learning benefits for their child, and usually correct	Deference to teacher's assessment
Pupil's learning needs more quickly identified	Pupil's learning needs vulnerable to being unidentified

ASIDE

CASE STUDY: ADDRESSING DISADVANTAGE AT COLERIDGE PRIMARY SCHOOL, ROTHERHAM

At Coleridge, our commitment to addressing disadvantage is grounded in the strengths of our school, community, families, children, staff and stakeholders. The school is located in Eastwood, an area that ranks in the top 1% nationally for deprivation, however we refuse to let this define or limit the potential of our students. Instead, we view this challenge as an opportunity to demonstrate that deprivation is never a barrier to progress. Our approach is focused on ensuring that every child has access to high-quality teaching and learning every day, beginning at the earliest stages of their education.

At Coleridge, our culture is the heartbeat of our school, driving everything we do. We believe that a strong, unified culture is essential for creating an environment where all children can succeed. This culture is built on the contributions and commitment of every staff member, each of whom plays a vital role in shaping our shared vision for the school. Together, we collaborate to produce the school development plan, ensuring that everyone understands not just what we are doing, but why we are doing it. This collective ownership and alignment around our goals fosters a deep sense of purpose and direction within our school community.

Consistency and well-established routines are the bedrock of the safe, purposeful environment we have cultivated at Coleridge. These routines provide our children with the stability and predictability they need to feel secure and ready to learn. By maintaining high standards and consistent practices in every aspect of school life – from classroom management to daily interactions – we create an atmosphere where children can thrive. This consistency is not just about discipline, it is about creating a nurturing environment where expectations are clear, and children know they are supported every step of the way.

Our culture of consistency extends beyond the classroom, shaping our interactions with families and the broader community. As the school is based in the centre of Rotherham in a diverse and multicultural community, it is key that our curriculum reflects this. Children and families thrive when they know that they feel a sense of belonging. This isn't tokenistic – there is a clear rationale and thought into the curriculum choices we make and the way we celebrate all faith events, in equal measure, to ensure every member of the school community feels represented and valued.

In our Early Years Foundation Stage (EYFS), we deliberately over-staff to create a rich, vocabulary-driven environment where children engage in frequent, meaningful interactions with adults through the SHREC approach (Share attention, Respond, Expand, Conversation). This method has proven to be transformative, enabling rapid progress for disadvantaged children and setting a strong foundation for their future learning.

To maintain the highest standards of teaching, we implement Instructional Coaching as a CPD tool. Every teacher is entitled to this high-quality CPD, working closely with a coach to refine and enhance their practice. *The Teaching and Learning Playbook* by Michael Feely and Ben Karlin (2022) guides this process, ensuring that coaching is low-stakes and empowering teachers with ownership over their growth.

We believe that relational behaviours are crucial in overcoming disadvantage. At Coleridge, we invest deeply in relationships, not only with our children but also with their families. Our commitment to being present for our families is evident in the time we dedicate at the start and end of each day to listen and offer support. This approach ensures that families feel valued and understood, fostering a sense of belonging and love that is essential for our children's wellbeing and success.

Our dedication to our community extends beyond the school year. Each summer, we run a HAF (holiday activities and food) club, which sees over 70 children participating. Their eagerness to attend reflects the strong sense of community and connection they feel with our school.

Assessment plays a key role in our approach to teaching and learning. We have developed a clear, six-step feedback process designed to provide all children with instant, impactful feedback. This approach is directly linked to our retrieval practices, where the next day's activities are informed by the misconceptions identified in previous lessons. These insights also guide our keep-up interventions, conducted by teaching assistants (TAs) each afternoon, ensuring that learning is retained in students' long-term memory.

When addressing attendance, we draw on Marc's insights into the power of pronouns, always choosing 'we' over 'you' in conversations with families. This simple but profound shift fosters a sense of collective responsibility and partnership. When overcoming barriers, like haircuts, public transport or medical appointments, our approach is always about how we, together, can navigate these challenges, reinforcing our commitment to being a united, supportive community.

At Coleridge, we believe that by harnessing the strength of our community, building strong relationships and providing high-quality teaching, we can ensure that every child, regardless of their circumstances, has the opportunity to thrive.

Ian Tankard

COMMUNICATION

Disadvantaged pupils thrive when schools focus on high-leverage approaches that respond to their needs and help them both academically and socially. Effective implementation is key to success. Supporting pupils with communication and language – and focusing on social inclusion – is something that can be enacted in all aspects of school life. It is something that all staff can take responsibility for.

Building pupils' communication and language supports success in the classroom. It supports the building of friendships and helps pupils manage unstructured times. (Play leaders, midday supervisors, sports leaders, etc. can all take ownership around social inclusion here.) Pupils of all ages are often like bees around nectar when teachers and other staff interact with them during unstructured times.

The development of communication skills and language skills also supports pupils' participation in enrichment activities and clubs. Disadvantaged pupils may need confidence to consider taking part in a new activity, as well as help to cover any costs. Email invitations are unlikely to draw in the least-confident pupils. Personal invitations, rooted in social inclusion and relationships, are far more effective.

Building communication and language skills also helps pupils to manage their social and emotional wellbeing. It can enable them to step into student leadership roles. Good communication as a leader doesn't just mean making speeches to participate but also involves developing listening skills. Many careers have communication and language at the heart of the role.

THE A–Z OF ADDRESSING DISADVANTAGE

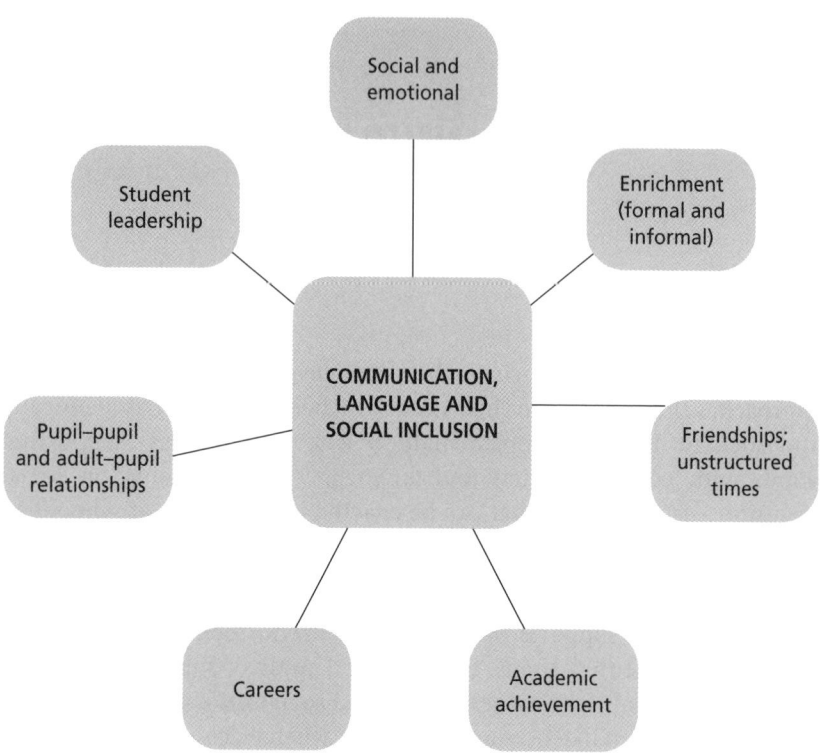

The importance of good communication skills

THE LINK BETWEEN THE LANGUAGE GAP AND SOCIOECONOMIC DISADVANTAGE

The language gap and links to socioeconomic disadvantage are well documented.

As Waldfogel and Washbrook identified in their 2010 report for The Sutton Trust ('Low income and early cognitive development in the UK'), when it comes to vocabulary at age five:

- There is a 27% gap in vocabulary development between pupils in the lowest income quintile and those in the highest.
- Those in the lowest quintile are 16% more likely to have problems with behaviour and 15% more likely to have problems with hyperactivity when compared with those in the highest quintile.

A language gap, coupled with social isolation (driven by social, geographical and in-school factors, such as difficulties making and sustaining friendships or over-intervention) has been identified in many of our schools. It may start in Early Years and grow over time.

ADDRESSING THE LANGUAGE GAP

Every moment in school needs to be a language development and comprehension moment. The presumption of language can leave pupils isolated in the classroom. Language is key to success in accessing the curriculum, in participating in lessons, in developing background knowledge that binds learning together, and in developing relationships with adults and peers. Oral language, in particular, is a key indicator for future academic success.

Equality of opportunity, valuing everyone's contribution in lessons and encouraging pupils to talk builds confidence and informs the teacher about misconceptions. Assigning pupils roles during classroom/partner talk and activities will help to ensure that all participate and take individual accountability. Support staff should refrain from talking to individual pupils during teacher input.

> In the classroom:
> - Are all pupils taught and expected to speak with confidence and clarity?
> - Are pupils given thinking time before embarking on discussion?
> - Are pupils taught to develop their listening skills?
> - Is pupil talk structured and teacher-led to secure opportunity and equity?
> - Are pupils accountable for purposeful talk?
> - It is conversation, not word exposure, that builds literacy and language.

Language comprehension facilitates independence in learning. It helps to ensure pupils do not opt out and contributes to belonging. It builds self-esteem and confidence. It can help all aspects of school life. Lessons where pupils struggle with language comprehension become something to 'get through', rather than to engage with.

It is important for subject and phase leaders to consider the impact of underdeveloped language comprehension on disadvantaged pupils in their areas of responsibility.

One of the biggest challenges for disadvantaged pupils locally and nationally is the presumption of language comprehension. As Beck et al. (2013) identified in *Bringing Words to Life*, we deepen knowledge through robust vocabulary instruction, not simple word exposure. This can be done by:

- introducing new words in interesting, familiar, child-friendly contexts
- not relying on dictionary definitions
- enabling pupils to interact with words in different, interesting contexts
- enabling pupils to have multiple encounters with new words
- testing whether pupils can use new words in different contexts
- rewarding the use of new words.

Bringing Words to Life, and the subsequent work it inspired, is so important for our disadvantaged pupils because it shows that addressing this issue is perhaps harder than we think – word exposure alone is not enough. But the rewards for doing so are significant.

Language and communication are about far more than academic achievement. A command of language builds emotional wellbeing, social interaction and friendships. It is at the heart of our development as humans. By developing a pupil's language and communication, we set them up to have positive lives. While language is often a focus in the Early Years, this needs to continue right through all key stages, as the evidence indicates that it remains a focus in all learning in all key stages.

- By addressing the language gap, intervening early and sustaining our focus, we can help to ensure that socioeconomic disadvantage and underachievement are not inevitable.
- Dictionary definitions are unlikely to help pupils who are struggling with language comprehension. Conversation, not word exposure, builds literacy and language.

- Pre-printed vocabulary lists and overwhelming word walls are likely to widen gaps, with pupils trying to please their teacher by using the longest word. Far more effective is introducing language to pupils together in interesting, pupil-friendly contexts.
- During classroom talk exercises, carefully plan the learning experience through the lens of the least confident learners. All too often, during class discussion exercises, disadvantaged, low-attaining pupils are left behind.

It's important to note that being successful with communication and language is not about speaking in a particular way. It is not about speaking with received pronunciation. It is about adaptability with language. Pupils who are successful with communication can evolve their language to the environment and situation they are in. They will adapt communication when speaking to their friends, teachers, senior leaders and visitors to school. Adaptability is key. Early years foundation stage is key to success. If children with under developed language start paired up with an adult rather than a peer, that may set the tone for academic and social isolation. The British Cohort Study suggests verbal skills at five are strongly associated with stronger academic and wellbeing outcomes into adulthood. (Centre for Longditunal Studies, May 2018)

We will interact with many words across the curriculum. For consideration:

Why might some pupils know these words?
Why might some mispronounce these words?
How might pupils react to mistakes?

'Ballet'	'Salmon'	'Cliché'
'Hyperbole'	'Anemone'	'Suite'
'Xenophobia'	'Worcestershire'	'Parliament'
'Debris'	'Epitome'	'Viscount'
'Specific'	'Arkansas'	'Subtle'

- Cost of living
- Cost of opportunity
- Social/geographical isolation
- New to English
- Poverty
- Unsociable work patterns
- Lack of transport
- Physical / mental health
- Feeling of belonging
- Societal judgements
- Peer influences / judgements
- Only interacting with words in print
- Only interacting with words once
- Limited talk at home

ASIDE

CASE STUDY: ADDRESSING DISADVANTAGE AT CAPEL MANOR PRIMARY SCHOOL, ENFIELD

Context and reasons for our journey

The starting point for developing our school strategy for addressing disadvantage was a recognition of the steadily increasing levels of deprivation being experienced by members of our Capel family. We were also seeing an increased attainment gap between our disadvantaged and non-disadvantaged pupils which clearly reflected the well-documented links between disadvantage and underachievement in the education system.

Our commitment

Underpinning our actions was the firm belief that, with a consistent and focused school approach, we *can* change the narrative for our children. This belief was coupled with a collective commitment to ensuring that the levels of disadvantage that impact them in their primary years do not define their futures. Caring relationships, high expectations and an ethos of collective aspiration were already embedded within our school culture and would provide a firm foundation for this approach.

Assessment and identification of need

In order to ensure that we were effective in addressing the impact of disadvantage for our pupils at Capel, we needed to pinpoint the specific area of need that was having the most significant contributory role in their underachievement.

Ongoing self-evaluation based on observation, assessment and question-level analysis identified the following:

- Low attainment on entry to Reception specifically linked to language and communication.
- Weak language and communication on entry across all year groups.
- Percentage of pupils with English as an additional language (EAL) well above national average.
- A higher number of incorrect responses in reading assessments when linked to understanding of word meaning and pupils' ability to summarise ideas in their own words.

Our findings reflected long-established research establishing an entirely logical correlation between disadvantage, vocabulary and achievement. This provided us with a clear direction of travel.

Developing our Capel approach

Placing vocabulary and oracy at the heart of school improvement, our disadvantaged strategy, school curriculum and classroom practice allowed us to develop shared understanding and aspirations which, as a result, led to consistent and robust implementation.

Intended outcome	Success criteria
Improved vocabulary and language for disadvantaged pupils	Observations show disadvantaged pupils increasingly using and understanding key vocabulary in their lessons. Pupils are able to use language to reason and to express themselves coherently. Assessments show improvement in reading comprehension. Assessments show improved language and communication following speech and language intervention.

Curriculum drivers

- Values
- Vocabulary and language
- Aspiration
- Breadth of experience

Addressing disadvantage: A four-pronged approach

- Vocabulary and language
- Curriculum engagement
- Reducing financial disadvantage
- Pastoral: relationships and emotional wellbeing (social, emotional and mental health (SEMH))

A snapshot of the school disadvantage strategy

Drawing upon research and providing related training for all school staff enabled us to develop an increased depth of understanding and expertise as a professional community as well as integral collectivity in our approach.

Implementation

Implementing our strategy has been a journey of multifarious actions including:

- self-evaluation and action planning
- developing a leadership role specific to vocabulary and oracy to ensure ongoing priority, development and continuity
- considering and discussing shared meanings and what we are trying to achieve

- developing shared expectations and non-negotiables such as the STAR approach (situation, task, action and result), while encouraging the individual freedom to explore the effectiveness of a range of strategies in the classroom
- identifying prioritised tier 2 vocabulary (high-frequency words used across a number of subjects) and tier 3 vocabulary (terms that are more subject specific) linked to the school curriculum
- developing pupil engagement and celebration of success
- developing resources and prompts such as lanyards for the EYFS staff
- developing familiarity with and cascading tried-and-tested learning strategies such as 'Accountable Talk'
- embedding expectations for explicit teaching of vocabulary within our reading structure
- developing a Capel Progression document of defined year group 'expectations for talk'.

Monitoring implementation

Expectations for teaching and learning within the classroom are regularly shared to ensure that vocabulary and oracy remain on the agenda and are incorporated within monitoring. Every monitoring visit to the classroom is followed by a meeting with selected pupils to discuss their learning and check whether they are able to understand and articulate the learning that has taken place and are able to understand and use the key vocabulary taught.

Impact

Analysis of data so far has not only shown a positive reduction in gaps between disadvantaged and non-disadvantaged pupils in key stage (KS)1 and KS2 but has also shown an impact for the attainment of all pupils.

External review has also shared that 'pupils readily engage in learning discussions using subject-specific, high-level vocabulary with confidence. They are able to articulate the meaning of challenging words, enabling them to access difficult texts and understand vocabulary linked to subject-specific areas.' This has led to accreditation for an area of excellence in 'Enhancing pupil outcomes through effective vocabulary development' (Challenge Partners Report, 2024).

The end … not quite!

Despite the evidence of impact that is already apparent, these are early days. Planning for sustainability and continued impact necessitates an ongoing process of self-evaluation and action planning to ensure that we are always alert and responsive to the individual as well as collective learning needs within our dynamic school community.

Marianne Enchill-Balogun

DATA

Despite considerable efforts by schools, the attainment gap remains stubbornly wide.

National data from the Education Policy Institute 2024 annual report shows the following data:

SECONDARY SCHOOL

One-quarter of pupils are defined as disadvantaged by the end of secondary school, a smaller proportion than at the end of primary school. This is because, as children get older, their parents are more likely to enter work and exceed the earnings threshold for FSM eligibility.

By the end of secondary school, the disadvantage gap widened from 18.8 months in 2022 to 19.2 months in 2023. Similar to trends in the primary phase, the disadvantage gap at the end of secondary school is at its largest since 2011. Following good initial progress in narrowing the gap between 2011 and 2014 (from 19.7 months to 18.2 months), the gap then remained at around 18 months in the years leading up to the Covid-19 pandemic. The gap is now 1.1 months larger than prior to the pandemic.

PRIMARY SCHOOL

29% of pupils are classified as disadvantaged by the end of primary school. In 2023 the gap between disadvantaged pupils and their peers at the end of primary school was 10.3 months, a similar size to 2022. This means that the gap is still over a month wider than it was prior to the pandemic and remains at its widest since 2011. It's important to note that, although the disadvantage gap has widened considerably following the pandemic, it was already beginning to widen in 2019, prior to the pandemic.

There are some mitigating circumstances. In their report, the Joseph Rowntree Foundation (2024) sets out how public services have been 'staggering under the weight of hardship'.

However, it is not helpful to assign the lack of progress in addressing educational disadvantage entirely to external factors. This handbook aims to support schools to do even better by their disadvantaged pupils, so they have the same opportunities to thrive as those from higher-income households.

This guide is not a list of things to do. It is a book built on what is happening in schools and classrooms where disadvantaged pupils are consistently thriving.

ASSESSMENT NOT ASSUMPTION

Diagnostic and formative assessment should shape strategy and activity for addressing educational disadvantage, not labels. Pupils are not at risk of underachievement because they are 'Pupil Premium'. They are at risk of underachievement because of the impact of low family income on their lives and learning over time. This is a process not an event.

Understanding the impact of low family income on learning and opportunity is key to success. Take time to ensure that any assessment is meaningful and useful to teachers and leaders.

Schools should ensure that assessment is used to adjust teaching responsively. This enables staff to respond to, and address, gaps in learning. Pupils then develop belief in themselves through experiencing success in the classroom and in wider school life. This helps them to become successful learners. They will believe that they can, and know how to, achieve well in tests and examinations.

Assessment, not assumptions, should inform our approaches. We need to properly understand the impact of disadvantage on learning. A poorly identified need leads to a poorly identified activity, which leads to weaker results and initiative fatigue. It can lead to a 'Supermarket Sweep' approach to addressing disadvantage. To quote Margaret Mulholland, a specialist on SEND and inclusion, 'We need to be experts in our pupils, not experts in labels.' Having effective mechanisms for sharing

DATA

meaningful information about pupils in a confidential, manageable way is one of the great challenges for addressing educational disadvantage. While there are lots of examples of this in the primary phase, there are fewer in the secondary phase. Greenshaw High School, in Sutton, Surrey, is one of the best examples. See strategy section for more.

The key for school leaders, and the whole school community, is to understand the impact of socioeconomic disadvantage on learning for the individual. Limited progress of pupils or poor attendance are symptoms rather than the issue itself. A strategy stands or falls on the understanding of this.

Diagnostic assessment (pastoral and academic), pupil voice, parental voice and teacher voice should all be used to inform our approach. It is important to avoid generalisations such as 'low levels of literacy'. Pupil need should be more nuanced.

It is important to focus on the causes of underachievement linked to disadvantage – such as oral language, background knowledge, self-regulation – rather than generalisations.

Data matters!

Tiffnie Harris, Association of School and College Leaders data specialist, said:

> 'In the commercial world, data is often described as the new gold, but in education, it holds even greater value because it helps us reduce inequality. Schools can draw on a rich array of data – ranging from assessments and teacher observations to behaviour, attendance reports and pupil wellbeing surveys – to build a comprehensive picture of the challenges faced by disadvantaged and vulnerable pupils.
>
> This enables early identification of needs, the implementation of tailored support and continuous monitoring to ensure interventions are effective. Accurate, targeted use of data is essential for improving outcomes and closing educational gaps between these young people and their peers.'

> # ASIDE
> ## CASE STUDY: ADDRESSING DISADVANTAGE AT NORMANTON JUNIOR ACADEMY, WAKEFIELD
>
> Normanton Junior Academy is a school where all our children belong, regardless of their starting points, barriers or challenges.
>
> It is about our children feeling safe, secure, happy and healthy so they are ready to learn.
>
> Our intention is that *all* pupils, irrespective of their background or the challenges they face, make good progress and achieve their potential across all subject areas. We want all pupils to want to come to school, be their best and be confident, independent, successful learners. The focus of our PP Strategy is to support disadvantaged pupils (any pupil at risk of underachievement) to achieve these goals and provide them with a range of opportunities which prepare them for the next stage of their education.
>
> We are intently focused on working on key priorities in a simple, systematic and effective way. Leaders, therefore, integrated both our Academy Improvement Plan and our previous PP Plan into one three-year strategy which focuses on overcoming challenges faced by disadvantaged learners, for the benefit of all. The format is an adapted logic plan, with simplified terminology, accessible and understood by all stakeholders. This has been transformational for our school improvement journey.
>
> We consider the challenges faced by vulnerable pupils, including children in care, those who have a social worker or those with SEND, and provide a clear pastoral offer.
>
> High-quality teaching – every day, for all – can, and will, make a difference.
>
> High-quality teaching is at the heart of our approach, with a focus on areas in which disadvantaged pupils require the most support and this has been a priority

for our school over recent years. This is proven to have the greatest impact on closing the disadvantage attainment gap and, at the same time, will benefit the non-disadvantaged pupils in our school. Developing teaching practice, over a sustained period, is driving meaningful change in our setting. This approach means all children are taught the same curriculum and content; all children receive an equitable offer with the same opportunities. No child in our school is going to feel different or that they can't achieve if they are accessing the same offer as everyone else.

As a result, the targeted academic support provided at our school supports and complements learning; it doesn't replace it. We have a clear mantra that if an 'intervention' becomes an 'outervention', meaning the intervention is not **better** than what the quality-first teaching, in class, is providing — we don't do it!

We also continue to adapt our curriculum to prioritise teaching-and-learning gaps or issues around content which has not 'stuck' so that pupils can make sense of later work in the curriculum. A broad and balanced curriculum is vital for all our pupils.

Our approach is responsive to common challenges and individual needs, rooted in robust diagnostic assessment, not assumptions about the impact of disadvantage. The approaches we have adopted complement each other to help pupils excel. To ensure they are effective we:

- make sure disadvantaged pupils are challenged in the work that they are set
- act early to intervene at the point need is identified
- adopt a whole-school approach in which all staff take responsibility for disadvantaged pupils' outcomes and raise expectations of what they can achieve
- use evidence-based approaches that support our challenges, with a clear rationale as to why we are using this 'resource' or 'strategy', for example, how we are going to do this and what the clear impact will be.

Luke Welsh

EVALUATION

High-quality impact evaluation is fundamental to better outcomes for disadvantaged learners.

A robust process and impact evaluation framework should be adopted at the start of a strategy's implementation to enable school leaders to assess its effectiveness accurately. Changes and adaptations can then be made to activity and strategy where necessary.

Impact evaluation is about finding out whether activities and strategies have been successful, and why. It is not about proving that strategies and activities have been successful or finding evidence to justify decision-making. Decouple evaluation from accountability. Trying to prove an approach has been successful is detrimental to improved pupil outcomes.

Evaluation is fundamental to continuous improvement, for building a solid evidence base that will enable impact on pupils.

- Understand, not prove.
- Objectivity is really difficult, *but* vitally important.
- Monitor the impact of CPD in the classroom. It is not enough to 'hope' that CPD will be enacted.
- Look for impact on learners that is sustained in the classroom.
- Case studies are helpful if chosen in advance. (Don't just choose pupils that are judged most likely to succeed.)
- Activity does not equate to impact on learners (however important for implementation).

The following table includes a number of approaches that schools can use for evaluation. They include qualitative and quantitative measures, and short-/medium-/longer-term measures, from classroom observations to end-of-key-stage attainment. All have limitations, as set out below.

Success criteria	Short/Medium/Long	Qualitative/Quantitative	Strengths	Weaknesses	Improved by?
Outcomes of KS2 SATs (standard assessment tests)	Long	Quantitative	Objective Directly comparable	Difficult to determine cause impact from a single activity Responsive action difficult	
Observations of learning behaviours/language	Short/Medium	Qualitative	Can inform improvements in practice	Can be subjective, especially solo Requires understanding of the evidence	Clarity of focus Observation of pupils
Book study	Short/Medium	Qualitative	Can inform improvements in practice and interventions	Can be subjective, especially if without expertise	
Pupil voice	Short/Medium	Qualitative/Quantitative	Can inform improvements in practice and interventions	Pupils can be swayed by influential peers Surveys can be narrow	
Parental voice	Short/Medium	Qualitative/Quantitative	Can give different perspectives	Swayed by influential peers Some pupils find formal discussion hard Surveys can be narrow	

Success criteria	Short/Medium/Long	Qualitative/Quantitative	Strengths	Weaknesses	Improved by?
Observations of oral language	Short/Medium	Qualitative	Can inform improvements in practice and interventions	Can be subjective	
Vocabulary test scores	Short/Medium	Quantitative	Can inform interventions Directly comparable Objective	Not standardised Not academically validated	
Teacher interviews	Short/Medium	Qualitative	Teachers as the 'expert' in the pupil(s)	Can be subjective	
In-classroom assessments	Medium	Quantitative	Can inform interventions Comparable Objective	Quality can be an issue Influenced by quality of teaching Not standardised	
Pupil progress meetings	Medium	Qualitative/Quantitative	Teachers as the 'expert' in the pupil(s)	Can be subjective	
Standardised tests	Medium/Long	Quantitative	Can inform interventions Directly comparable Objective Academically validated	Influenced by quality of teaching Content may not be taught	

Impact evaluation goes wrong when we adopt any of the following behaviours:

1. Base our evaluation of improvement on the weakest datasets, so that we can claim credit for any small improvements.
2. Base our evaluation of improvement on the reactions of those delivering the plan.
3. Base our evaluation of improvement on selected colleagues that were the most enthusiastic about the strategy.
4. Use vague outcome measures from the start, making success easier to claim.
5. Use one set of favourable data or ignore any negative findings.
6. Use sets of data that avoid focusing on pupil outcomes.

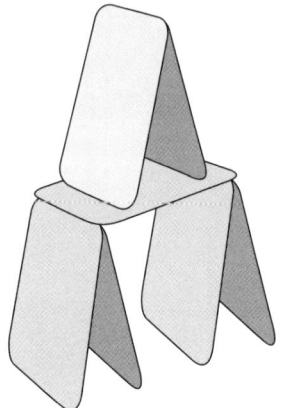

Poor evaluation: a house of cards

High-quality impact evaluation is fundamental to better outcomes for vulnerable learners. Evaluation is fundamental to continuous improvement and to building a solid evidence base that will enable the plan to impact on vulnerable learners. It should not be treated as an optional extra. It is part of good implementation. Set a clear evaluation framework at the start of the strategy, with short, medium and long term indicators. Use qualitative and quantitative measures. This is key to long term success for pupils. It aids better questions and discussions and supports psychological safety. A poorly designed evaluation framework leaves aims to individual interpretation, builds pressure and negates effective implementation.

> ## ASIDE
> ### CASE STUDY: ADDRESSING DISADVANTAGE AT COCKERMOUTH SCHOOL, CUMBRIA
> Here are some key things about our approach to helping all students to thrive, especially those who experience disadvantage:
> - **School values.** Ensure all staff understand them, live them and use them to make decisions. At Cockermouth, we worked together on defining what they mean and what they look like. We follow the acronym ICARE: include, community, aspire, respect, enjoy. We share these with students in assemblies and in our language day to day, including when things have gone wrong. This takes time, persistence and ongoing commitment.
> - **Know your students.** This is a basic expectation of all staff. It sounds obvious, but secondary schools are operationally complex. A teacher can see seven different groups in a day (form group plus six teaching groups), and each group could have up to 32 students. There's a big curriculum to deliver and it is hard to know your students well. You have to be deliberate at all levels. We give protected time for this and always reiterate the message. We have developed this into 'know *our* students now' — we think that's an important cultural shift.
> - **Careful implementation approach.** We use the EEF principles. Where we can, we take our time and we have trained heads of department (HoDs) in this too. We take time to explore the issue. We took the pressure off HoDs three years ago and gave them the autumn term to step back and really understand their areas before writing a development plan. We used £30k to get them together, off timetable, once a fortnight for leadership development. We can't afford that again at the moment, but it was pivotal in building shared values, understanding, common approaches, etc.

- **Leadership – authenticity.** We care about children, about every child, and that goes right to the top. We are out on duty every day before, during and after school. We are talking to children, to visitors and to staff. We want to know about what's going on in people's lives. It exhausts us – it would be easier to sit in the office and get lots of work done – but we want to know all those little things that make someone feel valued. We listen. We use the nuggets we pick up to know our community better and adapt to what is needed.
- **Leadership – no blame culture.** Mistakes happen; people get things wrong. We get things wrong. We learn, we get better.
- **Leadership – we are all learners.** Whether it's engaging with research, improving approaches or thinking about how we better ourselves, we are all learning. Our designated safeguarding lead (DSL) introduced us to 'professional curiosity' as a phrase. We have taken that beyond safeguarding – let's be curious about impact, about patterns, about anomalies, about what's not working. We should be curious about why and how we improve.
- **Deliberately making a positive culture every day.** Catch people at their best. Build relationships early. You will need them later because we also pick up what isn't working, but with respect and constructive support.
- **Pick the big things. For example, reading.** Some disadvantaged pupils who are low attainers have struggled academically and socially. The Thinking Reading programme has transformed their perceptions of themselves, their talk, their conversation, how they view themselves and how others view them.

I also want to caveat all of this with the fact that we are not there yet. We are a work in progress. We don't think we are getting it right for every child all the time – but we want to. Also, we haven't had one rigid plan. Some of this has evolved organically – and we've grown as people, as teachers, as leaders so it evolves further.

Dr Michelle Henley

FAMILIES

There is a strong association between parental engagement and good educational outcomes. However, research evidence about how to influence it is less strong. Evidence varies, depending on the age of the pupils. The key is defining what constitutes success with parental engagement, and ensuring that there is a collective understanding about this which is communicated to the whole school community.

Defining the aims of any strategy is vital. What does success actually look like? Can we, as a school community (including families), develop and settle on a shared understanding of parental involvement that is manageable, purposeful and rooted in evidence? Pupil success (in the classroom and wider school life) is a good driver of parental engagement.

Impactful approaches (that may be less complicated to implement) may include working with families to:

- speak positively about school and learning
- encourage them to show an interest in school and learning
- encourage good attendance, punctuality and behaviours
- promote good learning behaviours.

A headteacher in Ipswich once said to me: 'I know I have cracked parental involvement when my most vulnerable family is banging on my door wanting to know why their child has a supply teacher again!'.

EFFECTIVE PARENTAL ENGAGEMENT

We are often prone to adopting problematic proxies for effective parental engagement:

- attendance at parental consultations
- positive interactions through Dojo (an online communication platform), etc.
- completed homework
- reading records
- securing high-quality work experience
- enabling participation on trips, enrichment
- involvement in a range of activities at school
- involvement in PTA, school governance.

Effective parental involvement evolves over time, depending on the ages of the pupils. The following model should help:

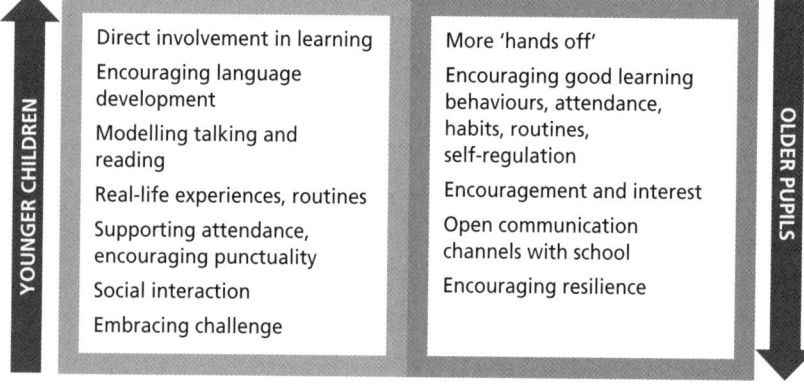

A model of parental involvement

Gill Main at the University of Leeds (2018) highlights how low family income can impact in hidden recesses of family life. To help disadvantaged pupils to thrive, we have to properly understand the impact of low family income.

> Children who were in a low-income household were:
> - 4.5 times more likely to have not eaten or not eaten enough when they were hungry
> - 5.6 times more likely to have had to wear old or poorly fitting clothes or shoes
> - 5.2 times more likely to have pretended to their family not to need something
> - 6.7 times more likely to have pretended to their friends that they did not want to do something that cost money
> - 6.7 times more likely to feel embarrassed by a lack of money
> - 4.4 times more likely to miss out on social activities.
>
> Their parents were 7.9 times more likely to have gone hungry. This points not only to the devastating impacts that poverty has on children, but also to the pervasive nature of ideas which suggest that poor people themselves are somehow to blame for their situation in life. Perversely, they are made to feel ashamed because they don't have the resources to have the same things and engage in the same activities as their better-off peers.
>
> **Gill Main**

The EEF report 'Working with parents to support children's learning' (2021a) contains some useful guidance on working with parents. Details can be found in the References section at the end of this book.

Stephen Tierney, formerly a system leader working in coastal Blackpool, has shared some high-quality resources on communicating effectively with families about attendance issues. More can be found here: https://leadinglearner.me/2017/07/02/absences-matter-and-you-can-help/

Research from the Resolution Foundation, published in 2023, highlights how families are increasingly poor and hungry, and consequently adopt 'short-termism' behaviours. Short-termism might mean families opt for payday loans, purchases on credit with poor interest rates, or more-convenient but less-healthy foods. It leads families to focus on getting through the day/week/month, as opposed to planning for the long term.

When a family is experiencing destitution, or any significant challenges or multiple priorities, it may also prioritise other issues over attendance to school or attendance to schoolwork, particularly home learning. As the teacher, I may recognise the long-term academic and social benefits of a curriculum trip, but critically low funds at home mean that paying to participate is not possible.

The Joseph Rowntree Foundation research (2023) goes on to suggest that 5.7 million low-income households were skipping meals in 2023.

The more stable a family's income stream, the longer ahead they can plan, whether for health, wellbeing, social or educational matters. Families on higher income streams are better placed to save for holidays (in school holidays), save for a child's university place, pay for books, and build social and cultural capital. Such families can also buy long-lasting, higher-priced clothing, and equipment that is more resilient. Families on the lowest income streams may be forced to buy less-expensive, and therefore less-robust, equipment, shoes, cars, etc. They will also have less access to cheap credit.

Food poverty can impact negatively on self-esteem, confidence, and health and wellbeing, and serves to drive social isolation.

Telling a family that is struggling to feed itself that it needs to plan for the long term may not always elicit a favourable response.

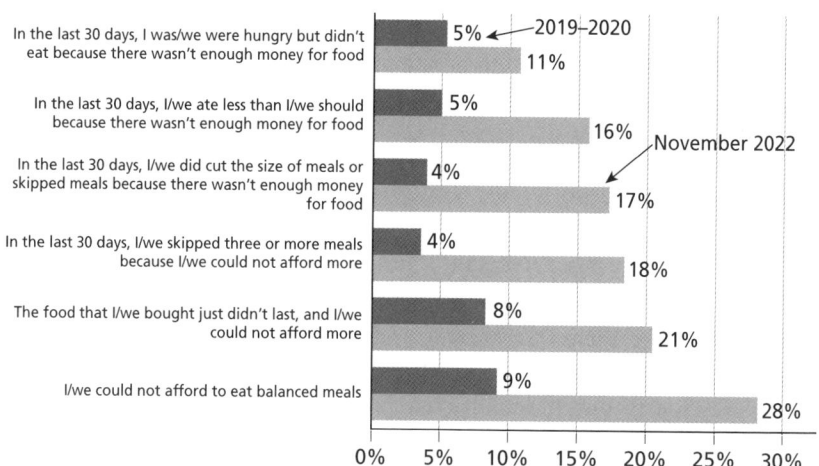

Comparing 2019–2020 with 2022 in terms of families struggling to afford sufficient food (from The Living Standards Outlook 2023 report, with thanks to the Resolution Foundation, resolutionfoundation.org)

The impact of low family income on pupils is a process, not an event. In some cases, this may start prenatally. It is a long-term issue that warrants a long-term response. Health inequalities mirror educational inequalities, which may impact on issues such as attendance. Low family income may also reduce opportunities for enrichment, travel, resources, books and more.

Access to the full curriculum, academic and personal development, should never be limited to those with secure/higher family incomes. Consideration of the economic wellbeing of families should happen at the curriculum-planning stage. This is true for the formal curriculum, educational visits and wider enrichment. If opportunity is limited to the ability, or willingness, to pay, we are exacerbating gaps.

It is important that low-income families are held in high regard by the whole school community. This should be non-negotiable. Pupils from low-income families need everyone in the school community to be their champions and their advocates. This is particularly important for families that might struggle to engage with the school community. Holding families in high regard should not be conflated with activities that take us away from the core business of school: learning and personal development.

Be wary of making judgements if pupils struggle to participate in enrichment activities or targeted academic support. See school life through the lens of the pupil.

HOW MIGHT LOW FAMILY INCOME IMPACT THE SCHOOL EXPERIENCE?

This can be broken down into three parts:

Pupils and families

A pupil's family background can influence a number of factors: oral language, vocabulary, language comprehension, gaps in background knowledge, self-regulation of cognition and emotions, dispositions towards learning, motivation, gaps in learning due to poor attendance and access to resources. Social isolation can be an important factor in the impact of disadvantage on learning: the more people we meet and interact with, the broader our vistas.

Community

It is important to consider the impact of growing up as a disadvantaged pupil within each school's community: cost of living challenges, geographical isolation, employment, transport, housing.

School

In-school factors that disproportionately impact disadvantaged pupils can include: cost of the school day/term/year, beliefs and assumptions, limited access to high-quality teaching, a failure to address the expectations of pupils and their families, high turnover of staff, lack of clarity in understanding the issues being addressed, initiative overload and poor implementation.

This is not an exhaustive list. These are generalisations. Have school leaders accurately assessed and understood pupil need in respect of how disadvantage impacts learning? Is there a collective understanding of this across the school?

Disadvantaged learners, those with SEND and those that are multilingual should not be treated as a homogeneous group. Labels can create unconscious bias and set limitations on what learners can achieve. Strategy and activity should always focus on pupil need.

Employ a proactive approach, anticipating future challenges and addressing them through early intervention. Early intervention is what we do in the moment, at the start of the school year ... It's about caring and responding to the day-to-day experiences of disadvantaged pupils in the classroom and in wider school life.

> ## ASIDE
> ### CASE STUDY: ADDRESSING DISADVANTAGE AT INSPIRE LEARNING PARTNERSHIP, SE ENGLAND
>
> We have to see schools as the heart of the communities we serve. Disadvantaged families need our hands wrapped around them so that we can encourage, support and love them. We need to see everyone that belongs to the school as our family.
>
> As with family, there is always a time where we must hold the boundaries and where we demonstrate 'tough love'. Not in a judging, harsh way, but knowing that this may help them. For example: 'It is not OK that XXX is at home. We must get them to school. What can we do to support them?'
>
> Relationships and a sense of belonging are key to our work with families. Families need to feel that we have 'got their back'; they need to feel that someone does listen, someone does care. We must model empathy and place ourselves in their shoes if we truly want to support our families.
>
> If we recall Covid-19, we remember that it was schools that were the civic establishments that families came to. Schools provided families with that much-needed lifeline. School was the place where people came to see a familiar face, ask for help or seek food. It was schools that made home visits or phone calls to families, giving them that human connection that we all craved at that time. Schools and teachers showed families that you matter and we care about you.
>
> Thankfully that time has passed but it reminded us that we are the lifeline for so many of our families.
>
> The key to our success when working with our most vulnerable families is making them feel that they matter. We need to love our families as our own.
>
> **Rupinder Bansil**

GROUPING

The grouping or setting of pupils is something that provokes much emotion and opinion. The issue is way too complex and nuanced for simplistic answers. This chapter aims to provoke some thinking to enable the reader to come to conclusions that are in the best interest of pupils.

THINGS TO THINK ABOUT

We should not think about the grouping of pupils as a binary issue: rigid setting/streaming versus mixed attainment. There are more nuanced approaches that can be adopted that can mitigate against some of the problems that either approach might cause.

Whatever approach we adopt, it is important that we involve teachers in the decision-making process, so that they feel agency – a done-with process, rather than done-to.

If we decide to go down the route of setting, we must be clear about the issues that are meant to be addressed by that approach. How will we know that we've been successful, particularly from the perspective of lower-attaining pupils?

It is critical that we involve pupils and parents in discussions around why grouping is taking place. Arguments for grouping can include: to enable students to experience success or to achieve personal excellence in the classroom. Be clear that it *isn't* because we want to separate them out from pupils that they perceive to be more clever than them. Not talking to pupils about why we are setting is one of the big problems with setting. If we don't explain our rationale, pupils will create their own narrative (which can be further baked in if family members had a difficult experience of school themselves).

WHY MIGHT WE WANT TO SET?

The following are all potential reasons why a school may decide to group pupils.

- We might have a very broad range of attainment in a cohort.
- There may be subject-specific issues.
- It may be that current practices with setting are leading to good outcomes for all pupils, including those with a low prior-attainment profile.

THE IMPACT OF GROUPING

It is important to think about the impact of grouping on:

- the expectations pupils have of themselves
- the expectations teachers have of lower-attaining pupils
- the quality of education experienced by the lower-attainers
- the perception of self that might come from being in a lower set
- the social isolation/effect on peer relations that might occur.

SOME PITFALLS TO AVOID

Some pitfalls include:

- grouping pupils based on a single assessment
- grouping pupils in a subject, based on an assessment from another subject
- having lower-attaining pupils working with non-subject specialists.
- grouping on anything other than current attainment
- grouping where lower-attainers are given easier content
- asking pupils if they like setting (it is much more helpful to ask them about self-perception and their attitudes to learning).

And a big pitfall to avoid: imposing mixed attainment teaching on teachers without prior discussion.

CLASS SIZE

Some schools are using PP funding to create smaller class sizes. While the evidence on the benefits of this is mixed, Blatchford and Russell's report *Rethinking Class Size* (2020) is very helpful.

Key to the success of this policy is to define the intended impact of smaller classes on disadvantaged pupils, and evaluate robustly whether or not they have been effective. Empower teachers with clarity about what is expected as a result of the smaller groups. By simply reducing the class size, but not codifying what's going to be different, we're unlikely to see the outcomes we'd like to see.

How might class size and grouping influence pupils learning behaviours?

Observations

- Do teachers give pupils the 'gift of their thinking'?
- Where in school do we see [disadvantaged] pupils develop good learning behaviours? Is this influenced by grouping or class size?
- Do pupils have ownership of their own learning?
- Is there any thing we do that negates good learning behaviours (check for understanding, presumptions of language, background knowledge, curriculum content coverage, TA interventions)?

Discussions

- What do we mean by good learning behaviours?
- What do we mean by poor learning behaviours? From wiping mini white boards to opting out of discussions to toilet passes…
- How can we improve learning behaviours (what's in our gift in school and in the classroom) – from SEMH intervention to oracy to front loading background knowledge?
- How will we (objectively) know they are improving?

ASIDE

CASE STUDY: SUPPORTING DISADVANTAGED PUPILS IN THE CLASSROOM: EVIDENCE BASED EDUCATION

I think it's important for teachers to know that there are a range of tools at their disposal to support disadvantaged pupils; they don't need to reinvent the wheel or do all the hard work on their own! Really, the single greatest thing teachers can do is to build their teaching expertise. The advantage to this is almost like a multi-pronged approach to support all students (and not just disadvantaged students).

This is why at Evidence Based Education, we built the Great Teaching Toolkit (GTT) to help teachers both in building their expertise and in taking this multi-pronged approach to supporting their students.

Three things that any teacher can do to support their disadvantaged pupils are to better understand individual needs, embed evidence-informed strategies into their practice, and build their adaptive expertise. The GTT helps teachers do all of these. The first is crucial because 'disadvantaged student' doesn't come with a blanket, automatic set of strategies to implement. Sure, on a macro level, we can see certain patterns and common traits, but this does not solve the individual needs of a single student in a classroom (although it can give us some possible hints).

We encourage teachers to take the GTT courses to learn about understanding students' needs, using quality assessment and leveraging the science of learning. And, in following the courses and exploring the resources in the GTT, teachers collect a set of evidence-based strategies they can implement.

Ultimately, it comes down to developing teachers' adaptive expertise. It's good to be an expert in knowing the challenges that many disadvantaged students face, but it's great to then adapt that effectively in response to the needs of a specific student in a given classroom. This takes time and, crucially, deliberate practice, which is exactly why we include structures in the GTT to promote embedding effective habits, working collaboratively with colleagues, and gathering feedback.

We know these are the hallmarks of effective professional development. Investing time and energy into professional development is, in turn, investing time and energy into our disadvantaged pupils.

C.J. Rauch

HOMEROOM

Every classroom is a child's homeroom, where they feel like they belong through academic and social inclusion.

Pupils who thrive in our schools tend to have …

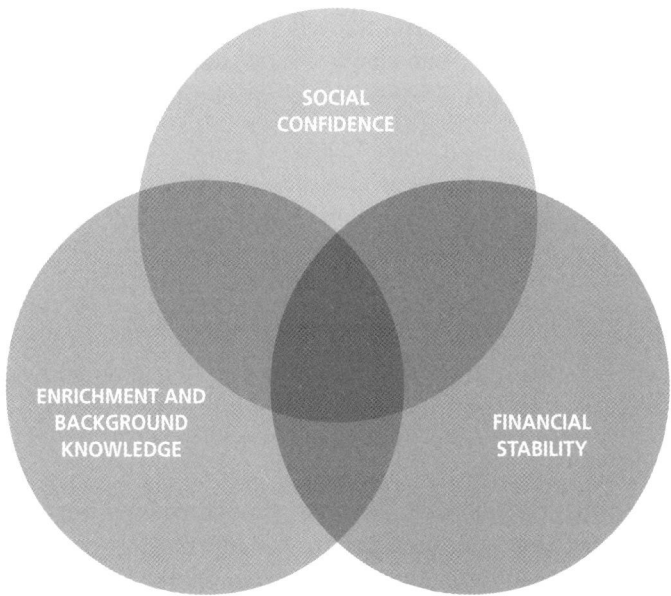

Schools are well placed to support pupils who do not necessarily have all of these advantages.

Thriving

Disadvantaged pupils thrive in school when there is a collective responsibility for a high-quality educational experience. These are underpinned by the highest of expectations in all aspects of curriculum provision, learning and personal development opportunities. Pupils from low-income backgrounds are more sensitive to the quality of education they receive.

Financial stability

Financial stability creates opportunity and choice. Low family income can limit those opportunities. Our disadvantaged pupils don't lack talent or ability, but they can lack opportunity. When we get it right, schools can be the great levellers in terms of academic learning, personal development and pastoral care. We do this by providing opportunities, but also by valuing everything that all children and families bring to our school communities. Life changes for pupils and families in school when they feel like they are positive contributors to their school and local communities.

Financial stability supports travel, access to cultural experiences, the capacity to save and plan for the long term (educationally and socially).

When children are growing up in lower income households, families are often forced to think short term. Low family income limits opportunity and confidence. It is expensive being poor – materially and socially. We can always prioritise things that will help our education or health and wellbeing in the long term, as we are 'getting through'.

Social confidence

A sense of social confidence is fostered through positive engagement in experiences. Schools provide a wealth of opportunities for interaction. As well as the countless interactions through the school day, such opportunities might include social interactions with people across the socio-economic spectrum through cultural experiences, work experience and co-curricular activity. These experiences are likely to be highly formative in growing a sense of belonging and enabling pupils to 'have the language' to support them in ever wider social contexts.

High quality enrichment opportunities may have a disproportionate impact on pupils from low-income families, who may lack opportunity outside of school. Many schools report that pupils from low-income families are less likely to participate, even when funded. It is important to ensure pupils feel included and that families are supported with economic wellbeing.

School leaders should be intentional about disadvantaged pupils being included in pupil leadership opportunities and playing prominent roles representing school in sports, music and community work. Positive experiences at school lead to motivation and belonging.

Careers education should start early and be of high quality. It should broaden vistas and build social capital. The quality of careers education (especially work experience) should never be limited to personal connections as this widens the disadvantage gap.

Enrichment supports pupils to feel like they are contributing to their own personal development, but also to help them feel like they are contributors to the school community. It therefore needs to be considered, planned and implemented with this in mind, rather than simply getting more disadvantaged pupils into clubs.

Enrichment and background knowledge: School life has the potential to enrich, broaden and extend the experiences that pupils already have. All pupils come to school with life experiences, however it is in the gift of schools to ensure provision secures equity for those who for whatever reason have had fewer, or more limited experiences of performing arts, sports, literature, film, pastimes, travel and more. 'Good' enrichment is activity that creates opportunity, broadens horizons, builds confidence, promotes social inclusion and belonging. It is particularly important for pupils who lack opportunities beyond school – but should not isolate or be only open to particular pupils. Quality opportunity should be available to all, low income families should not be excluded.

'Good' enrichment

This is activity that creates opportunity, broadens horizons, builds confidence, promotes social inclusion and belonging'.

It is particularly important for pupils that lack opportunities beyond school – but should not isolate or be only open to particular pupils. Quality opportunity should be available to all, low income families should not be excluded.

Levelling the playing field

How we level the playing field through front loading, and activating prior knowledge in an inclusive way is fundamental to success for disadvantage pupils.

The highest leverage approach for sustainably developing social inclusion, background knowledge and confidence is through improving pupils' reading. It's our greatest social justice lever.

Within our teams in school, we need to support pupils growing up in low-income households to overcoming these challenges and be socially included, always valuing what they bring to the community and celebrating their successes.

DO TEACHERS HAVE GOOD KNOWLEDGE OF PUPILS' LEARNING NEEDS, AND HOW IS THIS INFORMATION SHARED REGULARLY?

When staff have good knowledge of pupils' learning needs, adaptations to teaching and interventions more closely hit the mark. What do pupils know? What do they need to know next? This knowledge and its deployment are a key part of creating psychological safety in the classroom, ultimately leading to pupils feeling that they are 'good at this'.

Assessment of pupils' learning needs is a broad domain, and leaders need to be clear that assessment, monitoring and transition systems give staff actionable data to support pupils.

Here, we can briefly explore one fundamental aspect – that of checking for understanding. In his *Principles of Instruction*, Barak Rosenshine (2012) underlined that more effective teachers had strong checking-for-understanding protocols, asked lots of questions and evaluated pupil responses. He also outlined the wrong way to check for understanding: teachers calling on volunteers to hear their (usually correct) answers and then assuming that all of the class either understood or had then learned from hearing the volunteers' responses.

When teachers aren't investigating the difference between 'I taught it' and 'they learned it', many pupils can feel left behind and unheard. It is too often the case that pupils with a weaker understanding sit through lessons compliant but inhibited and fearing exposure. Pupils who regularly experience this may avoid coming to school.

The following table is a maturity index for checking for understanding.

From …	To …
Pupils show evidence of learning (e.g. mini-whiteboards, utterances) but there is too much information for the teacher to process or action.	Teacher has clarity over what they are looking for and engineers checking so that this is revealed.
Teacher takes responses from the most confident pupils.	Teacher uses different means of participation to elicit data which enables responsiveness.
Errors are difficult to respond to.	Errors are seen as valuable and interesting.
Correct answers are met with positivity, giving secret signals that pupils should only speak up when they are certain.	Teacher values thoughtfulness and effort. Contributions are met with emotional evenness.
Misconceptions can be left hanging.	Misconceptions are exposed and responded to.
Learning as a linear process, covering the curriculum.	Learning as a contingent process.
Core concepts and knowledge are covered.	Core concepts and knowledge are learned more accurately, rehearsed, discussed and interrogated.

Labels can get in the way of thinking about learning needs. A pupil with a diagnosis of autism who is also finding learning challenging might need glasses rather than having all of their learning needs positioned in relation to their autism. To quote Margaret Mulholland, we need to be experts in our pupils, not labels. SEND diagnoses must not cloud responding to observable, diagnosed learning needs (for example: they now need to learn their 5× table; they now need support in constructing a cohesive paragraph).

DO TEACHERS HAVE THE EXPERTISE AND SUPPORT TO MEET PUPILS' NEEDS? DOES PROFESSIONAL DEVELOPMENT ENABLE TEACHERS TO CONTINUE TO IMPROVE?

More now than ever, we have descriptions of how to implement and sustain professional development, including the work of education researcher Sam Sims. The 'what' and the 'how' of teaching are vast and complex, meaning that teachers' professional development needs are huge. It is imperative to use time impactfully.

Within professional development, teachers should be guided to prioritise key aspects such as reading diagnostics (phonic knowledge, fluency of reading) and the core mathematical concepts outlined in the DfE's 2020 'Mathematics guidance' (the so-called 'ready-to-progress criteria'). Backwards planning units of work can help teachers to grasp the journey they will take pupils on, and therefore what knowledge to prioritise and check along the way. Professional development should support teachers to avoid the trap of narrowing the curriculum as a result. Assessment tools are not a curriculum, and teachers should be supported to understand this difference.

WHAT SYSTEMS ARE IN PLACE TO SEEK AND HEAR PUPILS' VIEWS? IS THIS USED TO HELP IDENTIFY POTENTIAL BARRIERS TO PUPIL LEARNING AND ENGAGEMENT?

The 'curse of the expert' makes it hard to stay conscious of how a novice learner will experience content for the first time. Failing to view our classrooms, learning content or paired talk from the perspective of pupils can mean that there are barriers to engagement of which we are unaware.

We may be using words pupils don't understand. It may be that rather than I do > we do > you do, our pupils will feel that they really get it with I do > we do > we do > we do > you do. It may be something as simple as 'I can't see the board'. (I recently saw wonderful examples of this from Kirsty Bailey and Claire Davidson - in separate schools in Workington, Cumbria - holding pupils, walking them through the learning, building their confidence with every interaction so that the least confident, most quiet pupils experienced meaningful success within challenging learning. A joy.)

How do you ensure that you are successful in your learning?	
From:	To:
• I don't muck about.	• I ask for a better explanation.

How do you know that you have been successful in your learning?	
From:	To:
• I do well in a test. • I get a good grade. • I wrote a lot. • My lessons are fun. • I get rewards.	• I understood the teacher's explanation. • I checked my answers. • I used the example the teacher used on the board. • I asked a friend to check through my work • I have asked questions.

What do you do when you find a task difficult?	
From:	To:
• I put my hand up and wait for the teacher. • I get embarrassed.	• I look at the example the teacher has used. • I use the times table grid to help. • I ask questions. • I go back through my book. • My teacher asks someone to give an explanation about how they got to their answer.

What more could teachers do to support your learning?	
From:	To:
• Make lessons more fun. • Give you rewards.	• Slow down. • Give clearer explanations. • Encourage me to ask questions. • Tell me to be independent when I haven't understood. • Get pupils to explain how they got their answer. • Not sit me by my friends.

Without listening to our pupils, teachers may invest a great deal of time in preparing lessons which are ineffective without knowing why learning is failing.

The following websites and research papers may prove useful in this regard:

www.researchgate.net/publication/230853009_Teaching_Functions

https://educationendowmentfoundation.org.uk/education-evidence/evidence-reviews/teacher-professional-development-characteristics

www.aft.org/sites/default/files/Rosenshine.pdf

https://teacherhead.com/2021/10/17/check-for-understanding-why-it-matters-and-how-to-do-it-redsurrey21/

****

Teachers and other staff should have a shared understanding of the components of inclusive, quality-first teaching, specific to their subject and phase. Subject leaders and phase leaders should ensure that their daily practice, and that of the teachers in their teams, is inclusive and high quality for all.

There should be memorable, joyful learning experiences in which all learners, particularly the disadvantaged, are expected and encouraged to participate.

What can help is the professional development for teachers and other classroom practitioners that is focused on assessment of needs, as well as the recruitment and retention of specialist teachers. Disadvantaged learners may be disproportionately impacted by a high turnover of staff or difficulties in recruitment, as well as inconsistencies in expectations, relationships or knowledge of prior learning/experiences.

All pupils thrive when there is a relentless focus on high-quality teaching and a shared understanding of what this is.

THE USE OF INTERVENTIONS

Interventions might include:

- evidence-based interventions, such as the Nuffield Early Language Intervention
- small-group/one-to-one tutoring
- academic interventions to improve reading that can also be adopted in first-wave teaching. Academic intervention should supplement high-quality teaching, not replace it.

Any academic interventions should help improve learners as learners. They should be linked to diagnostic assessment and teacher expertise. Be wary of interventions looking for learners, rather than interventions that meet the needs of the learner.

The effectiveness of any intervention should be measured in terms of gains sustained in day-to-day learning. Be wary of the pre- and post-test fallacy, where learners make great strides but the impact falls away. This links to dispassionate impact evaluation.

Targeted academic support away from the classroom may be less successful when:

- Transitions to/from lessons are disjointed – especially when pupils have missed teacher explanations.
- Pupils experience curriculum narrowing and social isolation.
- There is a variation in the quality and expertise of staff leading interventions. High-quality, well-trained teachers and support staff are critical here.
- Interventions are disjointed from the curriculum. Chopping and changing of staff and routines can be harmful. It is better to be consistent and clear, so pupils feel safe and secure. Intervention staff are less likely to be redeployed when systems and routines are fixed. This ensures teachers are always clear about what learning has been missed when pupils are 'out'. We need to challenge received wisdom here. Better a consistent experience for pupils and staff. Intervention out of class is about trade-offs. The more an intervention

moves around the timetable, the less likely it is to be effective. If it is necessary, it should be prioritised and built on in the classroom.

The importance of early intervention

The earlier we intervene to support the academic and pastoral needs of our pupils, the more meaningful success they will experience. They, and their families, will enjoy school life and they will thrive.

The later we intervene, the more difficult it can be to address challenges. Pupils can become more conscious of the fact that they are being targeted for support and this makes it harder for them when they want to fit in. They become more aware of how they present to their peers. Materials published by the Early Intervention Foundation (www.eif.org.uk) can provide help and information. Early intervention is a consistent theme throughout this handbook.

Any interventions that involve learners being away from the classroom and their peers should be of exceptionally high quality, be rooted in research evidence and be a better learning experience than 'business as usual'.

Colleagues should work together, and engage in conversations that may feel challenging, for the benefit of learners.

Staff with the privilege of influencing the education of our most disadvantaged learners have to be their champions every day. They are a voice and an advocate for those learners in all aspects of school life.

ASIDE

CASE STUDY: ADDRESSING DISADVANTAGE AT HOPE PRIMARY SCHOOL, KNOWSLEY

A school with 88% of children living in the bottom 10% for deprivation and around 70% classed as disadvantaged creates certain perceptions and stereotypes. Our role at Hope is to ensure that when the children enter our school, they are accessing a high-quality, aspirational and ambitious environment.

One of our strong foundations for this is based around relationships. The influence an adult in school can have on a child can determine so much in their present and future achievements. A supportive approach is key for us, built upon positive behaviour and inclusive classrooms. A team of learning mentors supports pupils and families with a programme of pastoral support, including counselling, mentoring and family engagement, to address social, emotional and mental health needs. Children access a free breakfast club and there is a breakfast snack for those who do not attend. Positive school attendance is also vital to this approach.

From the start of a child's journey into school, there is significant investment in SEND support and speech, communication and language provision. Quality teaching and an ambitious curriculum offer is essential. We also invest in specialist teachers in a variety of curriculum areas. Educational visits and experiences play a pivotal role in bringing the curriculum to life and exposing pupils to the world around them.

We feel that the educational journey at Hope is memorable and one that enables children to maximise their potential both in the classroom and beyond.

John Casson

IMPLEMENTATION

EFFECTIVE IMPLEMENTATION

The quality of implementation should be as important as the activities and approaches chosen. Poor implementation is likely to lead to weaker outcomes. Prioritising and doing a small number of things well leads to shared ownership and understanding, gives time for approaches to be embedded, and avoids initiative fatigue. Implementation should be treated as a process, not an event.

Always consider some of the things that may go wrong before any implementation. Over-optimism is a consistent feature of failed initiatives. We should be enthusiastic about what we might achieve, but sceptical about how much we can sustain.

Some common challenges of implementation can include:

- underestimating time frames
- not involving the right people in training (avoid the 'cascade' model where possible)
- not having the right level of administrative support
- being unrealistic about how long things will take to embed
- not planning refreshers/updates
- over-reliance on an individual
- a lack of clarity over 'active ingredients'
- trying to implement too many things at once.

'Bad luck' has a greater impact when implementation is poorly thought through.

Avoid initiative overload. Draw on guidance on effective implementation.

Those involved in the implementation of any strategies are often poor judges of whether a strategy has been successful. The EEF's updated implementation guidance 'A school's guide to implementation' (2024a) will support efforts here.

ASIDE

GETTING IMPLEMENTATION RIGHT: CORNWALL RESEARCH SCHOOL

'A school's guide to implementation', published by the EEF (EEF, 2024a), is a guidance report that provides evidence and resources for schools to implement new educational approaches or practices effectively.

The guide is based on a new review of evidence and suggests three key recommendations:

1. Adopt the behaviours that drive effective implementation.
2. Attend to the contextual factors that influence implementation.
3. Use a structured but flexible implementation process.

The process is designed to support schools to do implementation, while the behaviours and contextual factors help schools to do it well. Research has shown that the quality of implementation is a huge factor in achieving the desired, positive outcomes from approaches. Even as more schools engage with research and evidence-informed resources and practices, the need to implement things well emerges as a high priority.

Therefore, the guide is intended to help ensure that new approaches or practices have the biggest possible impact on the outcomes of children and young people.

The guidance recognises that implementation and change are difficult and largely social in nature. Schools are complex systems in which it is vital that evidence-informed approaches are manifested in the day-to-day work of teachers, support staff and all who work in schools.

Recommendation 1 explores the crosscutting behaviours that drive effective implementation. These behaviours are:

ENGAGE
- Engage people so they can shape what happens while also providing overall direction
- Engage people so they have the potential to influence change
- Engage people in collaborative processes
- Engage people through clear communication and active guidance

UNITE
- Unite people around what is being implemented
- Unite views and values
- Unite knowledge and belief
- Unite skills and understanding
- Unite implementation processes

REFLECT
- Reflect, monitor and adapt to improve implementation
- Reflect on pupil needs and current practices
- Reflect on fit and feasibility
- Reflect on implementation processes
- Reflect on implementation barriers and enablers

Engage, Unite, Reflect

Implementation strategies that schools employ should allow and encourage these behaviours to be manifested. When done well, these behaviours can drive effective implementation.

Recommendation 2 suggests schools should attend to the contextual factors that influence implementation. These contextual factors are summarised in the table below.

What is being implemented?	Systems and structures	People who enable change
Consider whether what is being implemented is: • evidence-informed • right for the setting • feasible to implement.	Develop systems and structures that support implementation. They might include: • school structures, such as timetables • logistics and processes, e.g. data-monitoring systems • resources, funding, equipment • time, e.g. meeting time • policies • roles.	Ensure people who enable change can support, lead and positively influence implementation. Factors that influence whether people can support implementation might include the degree to which: • they have the knowledge, skills and expertise to help implement the intervention • they feel empowered to act and can empower others • they have agency.

School leaders should also reflect on the implementation climate of their setting. How people feel about implementation can greatly affect their ability to influence effective implementation.

Recommendation 3 advises that schools use a structured but flexible approach to implementation. Without a structured process, the crosscutting behaviours and contextual factors that underpin and drive effective implementation may be hard to enact. The guidance lists many implementation strategies that could be used by schools as part of a structured and flexible process. Schools should recognise that effective implementation takes time. Doing fewer things really well is a good attitude.

Effective implementation is difficult, but research shows that by enacting the behaviours and attending to the contextual factors that drive good implementation, schools can achieve sustained, positive behaviour change that will improve outcomes for their children.

John Rodgers, Cornwall Research School

JOB

LEADERSHIP OF PUPIL PREMIUM

There is a lack of consistency in leadership roles when it comes to leading on PP and supporting disadvantaged pupils. There is a lack of clarity over the expectations of the roles.

Roles can range from strategic leadership to specific work supporting individual pupils and families. The roles can also involve a focus on operational compliance, for example getting published statements uploaded.

The variability around the expectations, training, support and capacity can stymie systemic impact.

The following job description/person specification has been written based on how the role is enacted in schools where disadvantaged pupils are thriving and outcomes are strong.

The role would be enhanced by mandatory training, updated at regular, frequent points. This training should be quality assured, based on research evidence and good practice. The learning available to disadvantage leads should be consistent across the system.

PUPIL PREMIUM LEAD JOB DESCRIPTION/PERSON SPECIFICATION

- This person should sit on the senior leadership team (SLT).
- This person should have regular, frequent contact with those leading on teaching and learning, pastoral care and personal development, as well as curriculum leadership.

- The key purpose of the role is to engage and unite the school community around raising the attainment and wider outcomes for disadvantaged pupils, irrespective of the numbers of disadvantaged pupils in the school community.
- The PP lead should draft the school's disadvantage strategy, and then ensure that all stakeholders have an understanding, clarity and ownership over:
    - intent and ambition
    - challenges faced by disadvantaged pupils
    - intended outcomes and success criteria
    - activities to address challenges and the evidence that supports their use.
- The PP lead:
    - is responsible for the effective implementation of the school's strategy, and should work with other leaders around quality assurance of provision, ensuring that the voices of key stakeholders are heard.
    - should undertake the necessary training and support to ensure they have the relevant expertise in their role.
    - should seek out examples of excellent practice in contextually similar settings.
    - should commission an external review of strategy and provision where appropriate.

WHAT IS HAPPENING IN SCHOOLS WHERE DISADVANTAGED PUPILS ARE THRIVING?

Senior leadership teams in schools where disadvantaged pupils are thriving academically and socially:

- have domain-specific knowledge, both of strategy and activity
- are evaluative/reflective about the effectiveness of provision
- can lead and embed change (this is *hard*, especially when changing beliefs, assumptions and prior experiences)

- display empathy and understanding, but don't slip into sympathy/killing with kindness
- show commitment to evidence, coupled with building teacher knowledge agency and expertise (for challenging assumptions, not justifying decisions)
- focus on what is in their school's gift (they don't chase the wind).

The key questions to address, when considering whole-school priorities, cohorts, classes and individual pupils, if the attainment and wider outcomes for this (group of) disadvantage(d) pupil(s) are not improving, are:

- What will be done differently?
- What will be improved?
- What will be paused/stopped?'

Following the engage, unite and reflect process here, dispassionately, supports better outcomes for learners, benefiting the whole school community. The answer to addressing educational disadvantage is rarely to *do more stuff.*

Working with Governors is a key part of this role. Working with Patty Williams from the Education Research Alliance in West Cumbria, we developed the governors checklist:

Pupil Premium Governance Checklist

1. Is the attainment of disadvantaged pupils improving?
   - In school?
   - Benchmarked against non-disadvantaged pupils nationally?
2. Is the quality of teaching for disadvantaged pupils improving?
   - What are the objective measures that tell you this?
3. Has the school created a culture of inclusion and high expectations for disadvantaged pupils?
   - What are the objective measures that tell you this?

4. Have leaders identified the (controllable) academic and social challenges faced by disadvantaged pupils?
5. Is there a shared understanding of these challenges and the role of the school community in addressing them?
    - What are the objective measures that tell you this?

> # ASIDE
> ## CASE STUDY: ADDRESSING DISADVANTAGE AT WILBURY PRIMARY SCHOOL, ENFIELD
>
> At Wilbury, through leadership capacity, there is a sharp focus on the quality of pupils' learning experiences. Our leadership team plays a significant role in evaluating progress through ongoing, and crucially supportive, monitoring and quality assurance. Members of the team devote time to our staff for collaborative team planning, teaching and modelling by spending time in classrooms to provide on-the-spot coaching, training and immediate feedback to develop practice.
>
> The key to addressing educational disadvantage is to focus on the main thing: improving the quality of teaching on a daily basis, all within an open and enthusiastic culture where staff at all levels support and challenge each other in a spirit of professional improvement.
>
> *Never assume* that what you think is going on is going on! This is why you need 'out-of-class' leaders to be continually checking and supporting; every moment matters for our disadvantaged pupils.
>
> At Wilbury, the practitioner is the intervention. Our approach is one where we intervene immediately to improve the quality of our teachers and support staff. There are *no* labels put on our disadvantaged pupils. We know that their progress is dependent upon the quality of staff at all levels across the school.
>
> We are optimistic sceptics; we know we have our priorities right, but we also *never assume* and we keep *banging on*, day in, day out!

Addressing educational disadvantage is a whole-school approach not an event. In summary:

- Whole-school culture and intent are key.
- School leaders prioritise high-quality CPD and daily support from experienced teachers and leaders; quality assurance is key.
- School leaders have the confidence to be self-directed. We know our children and staff and are clear about our priorities; we have the confidence to say no to things that do not fit with these.
- We focus on fewer things and on doing them better.

Lisa Wise

KINDNESS

Kindness is not something soft or soppy. It is often much easier to be unkind.

RELATIONSHIPS

Efforts to support learners will stand or fall based on the quality of relationships we forge. Relationships between adults and learners, and between learners themselves, matter. To be successful, learners will need to feel like they belong in our schools and our classrooms.

Multiple studies have shown that where relationships across schools are strong, the most disadvantaged learners will thrive. Learners do well when teachers know them well and hold them in high regard.

Relationships are drivers of human development. The importance of positive relationships was highlighted by Osher et al. (2020):

> Relationships between and among children and adults are a primary process through which biological and contextual factors influence and mutually reinforce each other. Relationships that are reciprocal, attuned, culturally responsive, and trustful are a positive developmental force between children and their physical and social contexts. Such relationships help to establish idiographic developmental pathways that serve as the foundation for lifelong learning, adaptation, the integration of social, affective, emotional, and cognitive processes and will, over time, make qualitative changes to a child's genetic makeup.

Relationships between staff members matter too.

Good relationships should enable open, reflective discussions about the quality of the learning experiences of *all* learners in our schools and about the quality of personal development and pastoral care. They should enable discussions about any targeted academic support.

Colleagues should work together, and engage in conversations that may feel challenging, for the benefit of learners.

INCLUSIVITY

To support pupils learning, and in wider school life, there needs to be a more consistent, collective understanding of inclusion and inclusivity. Our work (*Addressing Educational Disadvantage*, 2021) found that this was variable in both theory and practice. To help address this, our guidance set out a maturity index and better proxies for inclusion.

Our system should mature in its inclusivity over the duration of the plan, from that which:

- identifies pupils as separate, requiring different resources and strategic approaches
- uses diagnostic labels to inform strategic planning
- sees labels as an anchor on attainment
- plans for 'most' and then 'some'
- uses bell-curve thinking
- focuses on operational compliance
- relies on individual experts
- relies on individual ownership of pupil groups.

Moving to a system that:

- recognises difference
- adopts inclusive pedagogy for all
- adopts a strengths-based discourse that celebrates difference
- expects to be surprised by pupil potential
- sees all pupils as their responsibility
- considers accessibility for everyone
- sees the purpose of education as social justice through better attainment
- focuses on inclusive teaching and learning
- develops system-wide knowledge, responsibility and expertise
- develops collective responsibility and ownership of pupil groups.

It is important to be wary of potentially poor proxies for inclusion:

- assigned responsibility
- pupils are in lessons with their peers
- pupils are being supported by a staff member
- pupils are busy and engaged
- work is differentiated
- pupils working in smaller groups
- work has been completed; there are answers in pupils' books
- additional interventions are provided
- nurtured vs attainment false dichotomy
- staff training has taken place.

It would be better if pupils are participating in and being successful with challenging learning over time through:

- teacher expertise: subject knowledge and inclusive pedagogy
- high impact practices (HIPs)
- HIPs and high expectations
- background knowledge (subject and pupil)
- modelling, scaffolding and worked examples
- collaborative learning strategies
- oral language strategies where pupils' contributions are valued
- consolidation and checking understanding (not rushing through content)
- assessment for learning
- evidence-based intervention.

A strength-based discourse around pupils and families is key to building a culture of inclusivity.

Research by Professor Stephen Gorard (2023) shows that the more that disadvantaged pupils are socially segregated, the bigger the attainment gap. Addressing this is something in our gift – at school and community level. This should be a priority and at the heart of efforts ahead. Many of the liaison group projects support this.

Social segregation is something to consider within school, and within classrooms too. Be careful with any grouping of pupils based on current attainment – setting or in-class grouping. This is also true when it comes to wider school life such as educational visits, enrichment activities, sports teams, pupil leadership, school productions, etc. Plan these opportunities through the lens of disadvantaged pupils.

Social isolation is likely to lead to increased levels of 'mirroring', where the behaviour of pupils subconsciously imitates the gestures, speech patterns, attitudes or behaviours of those around them. Social norms are a powerful driver of behaviours.

> **ASIDE**
>
> **CASE STUDY: AFFORDABLE SCHOOLS STRATEGY, WILTSHIRE LA**
>
> Cost of living can affect us all and beyond the label of Pupil Premium, we cannot be certain at any one-time which families, or members of our school community, are experiencing financial hardship. While every child attending school shares the same physical space, the way they experience school life and the feelings this generates may be very different if we think about it 'through the lens of affordability'.
>
> Through our Affordable Schools Strategy, we have witnessed a collective commitment to understanding the lived experience of disadvantaged learners in our schools. Our collaborative approach has given us the opportunity to work with a range of fantastic school leaders to develop innovative and effective strategies which promote inclusion and reduce poverty related stigma. This has resulted in universal, positive changes to school policy and practice, without limiting the quality of education on offer.

Leaders have been robust, creative and solutions focused when implementing this strategy, identifying key priorities and achieving many 'quick wins' along the way. For example, we have become much more aware of the impact of behaviour policies which sanction lack of equipment or non-compliance with costly uniform; the grim irony of requesting food donations for a Harvest Festival; the demands of multiple fundraising events and the cost of school trips and enrichment; the lived experience of a pupil in receipt of FSM at lunchtime - "Nothing says poverty like a brown paper bag".

Thinking through the lens of affordability is a hugely rewarding approach. 'Affordable Schools' have seen improvements in attendance, learning behaviours, pupil wellbeing, relationships, parental engagement and outcomes. As with every aspect of school improvement, positive actions to address the challenges of disadvantage benefit everyone and allow our school communities to truly thrive.

Kate Wilkins

LEARNING

For disadvantaged pupils to thrive, we need the following:

- To have clear and consistent expectations, routines and structures. All pupils feel safe and secure when they are confident they know what's coming. Structure liberates!
- To recognise that pupils are largely consistent in their behaviours and interactions with school and learning. The challenge comes when we, the adults, are the variable; when we are inconsistent. This may relate to recruitment and retention of staff; it may relate to micro-interactions in the classroom or around school. We are the variable; we need to be the consistent.
- To have an understanding that background knowledge is the glue that makes learning stick:
  - Build background knowledge to help pupils feel like they belong.
  - Frontload the key knowledge that pupils will need to be successful at the start of lessons.
  - Don't make presumptions about pupils' background knowledge.
  - Asking pupils to research subjects that many know little about is likely to be a gap widener.
  - Background knowledge is a huge driver of motivation. (For example, when *Romeo and Juliet* is introduced in a lesson, a learner might feel super confident if they have seen the ballet and been to visit Juliet's balcony in Verona. However, they are likely to feel less confident if they haven't, and even more so when they learn that their peers have.)

Teaching strategies should support independent, self-regulated learning though scaffolding. Pupils should be explicitly taught to plan, monitor and evaluate their work, emphasising and activating knowledge of self, knowledge of strategies and knowledge of task.

The strands in the EEF Teaching and Learning Toolkit that have the biggest impact on pupils are all things that improve pupils as learners:

- metacognition
- reading comprehension (our efforts to address disadvantage stand or fall on how well pupils learn to read and transition into reading to learn)
- oral language
- feedback.

The effectiveness of feedback stands or falls on pupils' perceptions of themselves as learners, and the relationship between the person giving the feedback and the person receiving it. If pupils have a negative perception of themselves as a learner, they may well find it more difficult to take on board feedback.

The impact of low family income on learning is not static; it is not a moment or an event. It is a long-term process. Knowing that a pupil is eligible for the PP will not give sufficient information to determine effective provision or intervention. Socioeconomic disadvantage may mean pupils:

- feel like they are on the margins of discussions
- do not have the background knowledge to make connections with learning; background knowledge binds learning together
- do not have the self-regulation skills (knowledge of self, knowledge of task, knowledge of strategies) to plan, monitor and evaluate their work
- have lower levels of oral language (a limiting factor on future attainment)
- have a more limited vocabulary, or difficulties with language comprehension, making it difficult for them to access lessons and sequences of lessons across the curriculum

- have a negative perception of themselves as learners, particularly if they get lots of focus on themselves on account of low attainment or being 'Pupil Premium'
- experience lower expectations through labelling (e.g. 'low ability' or 'Pupil Premium').

All of these things can impact on motivation, the beating heart of self-regulated learning. So, disadvantage in the classroom becomes self-fulfilling and can lead to problematic practice, such as differentiating down or focusing on task completion, rather than planning for learning and participation through strong explanations and scaffolding up through modelling and worked examples.

These issues impact on pupils across the socioeconomic spectrum, but they are more likely to impact on those from disadvantaged backgrounds. They do not occur because of any label, but they may present to pupils from disadvantaged backgrounds more often. It is important to focus relentlessly on the impact of disadvantage on learning.

Some issues faced by pupils may be beyond the school's power to change. But it is possible to address the impact these issues have on learning, as well as pupils' sense of belonging at school and in the classroom.

For all of our pupils, but particularly those who are disadvantaged, the most effective approaches to tackling disadvantage are not about big interventions, but countless small interactions, discussions and individual moments that create a sense of belonging for all. Self-esteem and pastoral approaches are about what happens inside and outside of the classroom.

Everyone in school should take responsibility for better outcomes for disadvantaged learners. It is vital that all staff understand:

- the issues being addressed
- how the school is addressing them
- the evidence to support that approach
- their role within that
- what success looks like.

The most effective strategies give teachers and other staff the capacity, expertise, knowledge and development to meet the needs of their pupils and improve them as learners.

Teacher agency and buy-in is fundamental to success. In addressing disadvantage, include and motivate, don't isolate. Nuance is key.

The following maturity index may support this.

Label led	Learning led
Marking books of PP pupils first.	Targeted feedback at pupils most at risk of underachievement.
Asking questions of PP pupils first.	Targeted questioning to check for understanding.
Free revision guides for PP pupils.	Targeted, structured revision support for those that lack opportunities for revision outside of school.
Seating PP pupils at the front of the class.	Careful seating plans to maximise learning.
Free trips and clubs for PP pupils.	Consideration of the economic wellbeing of all families, with targeted individual support. Prioritise FSM, especially long-term eligibility.
What are we doing to support our PP pupils?	How does [socioeconomic] disadvantage impact on pupil learning and participation in wider school life?

Long-term disadvantage will have a greater impact than periodic disadvantage. The longer a pupil grows up in poverty, the greater the risk of underachievement in the classroom and beyond, and the greater the impact on pupils' health and wellbeing.

ASIDE

CASE STUDY: ADDRESSING DISADVANTAGE AT ST CLARE'S CATHOLIC PRIMARY, ESSEX

St Clare's Catholic Primary School is part of the Rosary Trust and is situated in Clacton, Essex. The school has 314 pupils on roll aged 4–11 and has a nursery on site with 65 pupils on roll.

Clacton ranks among the top 1% of deprived neighbourhoods in the UK and we currently have 44% of pupils eligible for PP funding. The percentage of pupils with special educational needs is 17%.

Our ambitions

- To create the ethos of opportunity and success for all.
- To change the mindset of how we look at our disadvantaged pupils and our disengaged parents.
- To address the primary need of all our pupils in school.
- To develop the understanding of the staff about the importance of quality-first teaching and adaptive teaching strategies.
- To develop positive relationships between parents, staff and children.

How we work to those ambitions

We use a three-spine approach: teaching, behavioural and pastoral.

- We revised the PP strategy plan to ensure money was well spent on reducing class sizes and focusing on high-quality, high-impact support. Our ambition is for pupils and adults to be successful.
- We run a high-quality training programme; we invest in people not resources. This includes training an 'Expert' on the DfE's Covid-19 recovery programme.
- We employ a speech and language teacher, enabling us to offer Elklan Training speech and language support for 3–5-year-old pupils (Level 3) and support children with unclear speech (Level 3).

- We have a maths specialist teacher.
- The school has a Forest School lead teacher.
- Two members of staff have attended middle leadership courses (NPQML) focusing on maths and learning behaviours.
- Fidelity to our schemes ensures they are delivered as intended and achieve the desired results.
- We have addressed the primary needs of all our pupils ensuring a range of appropriate support, including a nurture room, a play therapist, a family liaison worker and an emotional literacy support assistant (ELSA).
- We successfully applied for an Inclusion Framework grant and use other funding opportunities to support the school's needs.

We work closely in local partnerships and with local projects. We have welcomed opportunities to work with external visitors, including the Essex Inclusion Review team, specialist SEND support, independent advisors, the LA and the diocese, to help support our vision and improvement plan.

We work collaboratively with other schools to enhance our curriculum with a focus on widening opportunities. We welcome parents into the school to value their child's achievements through showcases and informal meetings. This has been a journey for us resulting in higher attendance and support year on year.

Monitoring and evaluating

We track academic progress half termly and the SLT meets termly to discuss pupil progress.

- We use the six core strengths assessment tool for children with SEMH needs and the WellComm assessment for children on our speech and language register.
- Subject leaders monitor and evaluate their subject closely and make termly improvements.

- We act on feedback from specialists – formally and informally – and report findings regularly to governors.
- We review the results of our parent questionnaires and act upon the feedback.

Progress and attainment

At St Clare's we promote high expectations. Teachers are well trained and use evidence-based strategies which contribute to our successful outcomes.

The following approaches across the school have contributed to our successful outcomes.

- WellComm children leave EYFS with the confidence to speak to adults and peers. Their range of vocabulary has been extended and they are able to choose the correct word for the purpose intended.
- Use of the Schofield & Sims phonics scheme means that pupils' reading levels are in line with national reading levels in EYFS. In 2024, our phonics results at the end of Year 1 were 78%.
- Flexible interventions: we take this approach throughout the school to ensure a 'keep-up' attitude to learning.
- We follow a Maths Mastery approach that focuses on the six key areas of early mathematical learning.
- Herts for Learning (now HFL Education), a KS2 reading intervention proven to increase fluency.
- Development of a nurture room. For some of our pupils, the classroom environment was a challenge. Frequent dysregulation and instances of challenging behaviours have been minimalised through effective use of our provision.
- The Trauma Perceptive Approach (TPP). This is the basis of our holistic approach to meeting the needs of all children. All staff have been trained and CPD opportunities happen regularly to improve practice.

- Working with parents. Communication with our parents is key and through carefully planned support, we maintain strong, positive relationships between school and our families.
- Enriching the curriculum and creating opportunities. We work with a wide range of external, skilled professionals in order to enhance our curriculum and give unique opportunities to our pupils. This includes working with community coaches, The Royal Opera House, wildlife trusts, Young Voices and Colchester United football club.
- Working collaboratively. We have been given the opportunity to work with other schools and specialist support locally and nationally to gain the knowledge needed to advantage our disadvantaged, ensuring we prioritise opportunity for all.

We have found that our nurture room gives pupils a chance to succeed and have a positive school experience, allowing them to feel valued, understood and included. When children can remain in school, they have the opportunity to gain a better understanding of themselves and build on their self-esteem by working on a personalised timetable. This gives our pupils the opportunity to continue their academic progress through personalised learning both in the nurture provision and in class.

Outcomes

When our children enter EYFS, their levels of attainment are lower than average: 75% are below the expected standard. By the end of KS2, in 2023, 84.4% of our pupils reached the expected standard in reading, writing and maths, which is 24% above the national average. In 2024, 81.8% of our pupils reached the expected combined standard, which is 20% above the national average. For the last 6 years, our pupils have achieved results above the national average.

Jamie Whiteside

MODELS

Addressing educational disadvantage is not a problem, it is a privilege. However, it will require strong partnerships across our education community. This is true for everyone: all types of schools and their leaders, pastoral experts and curriculum leaders, Early Years practitioners and experienced secondary teachers, early career teachers and governors, system leaders, local authority officers and external organisations. It will need the acceptance that we can do better, not because we are doing badly, but because the effectiveness of our schools is best measured by how our educationally disadvantaged pupils perform. That *can* be better.

There are three models, given as A, B and C, that can be adopted by a school when starting to address disadvantage. They each take a slightly different approach.

MODEL A

This model was developed with Jon Eaton of Kingsbridge Research School.

The lighter boxes in our model are 'critical components'; they are all essential for addressing educational disadvantage. Without each of these components in place, any strategy to address disadvantage is much less likely to be successful. Responding to the drivers significantly influences the effectiveness of impact.

The DfE and EEF guidance refers to 'wider approaches'. This is too vague, and smacks of an afterthought. We know that even when disadvantaged pupils attain well, they are still less likely to get the higher education opportunities or career opportunities those grades would deserve. A clearly defined personal development curriculum that supports the learning of our disadvantaged pupils is fundamental to success. Similarly, disadvantaged pupils thrive when pastoral care is strong and consistent, particularly around attendance.

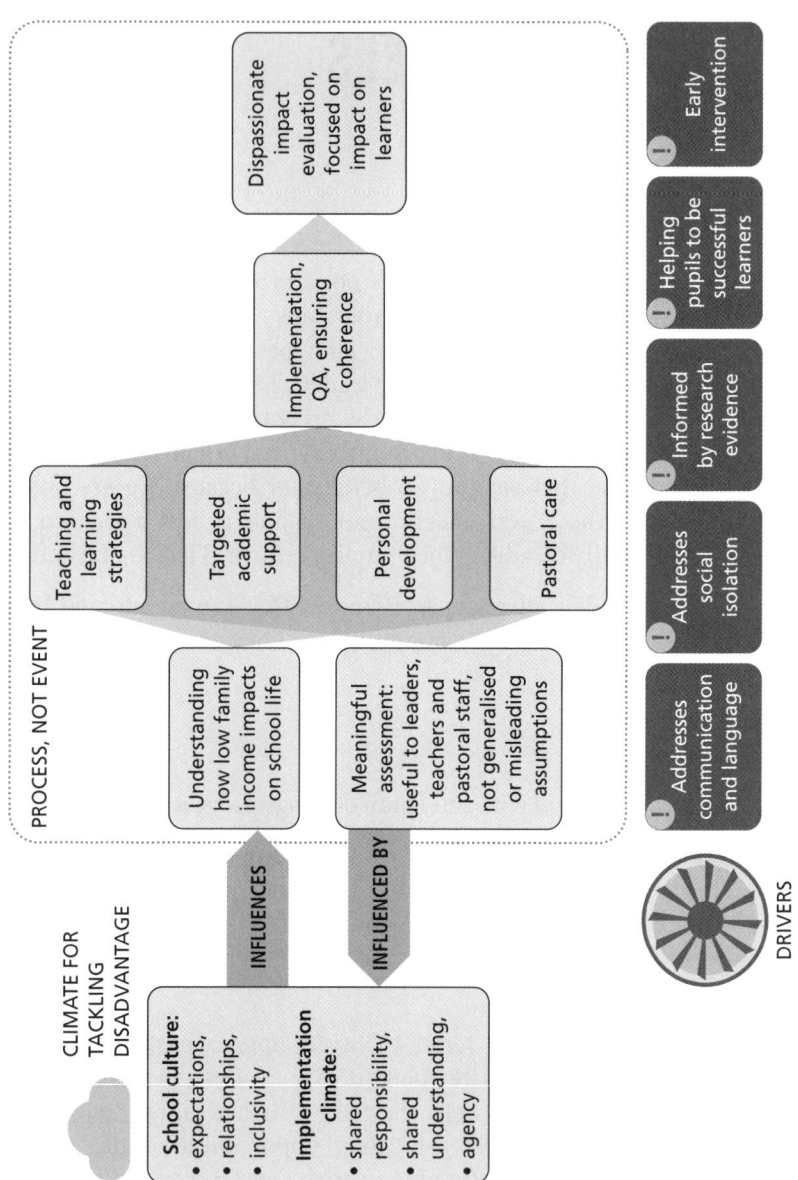

Model A

MODEL B

This is similar to model A, but puts provision front and centre, with themes that should inform that provision in the outer circles.

Model B

MODEL C

This model, developed with colleagues nationally, puts the pupils' experience in the classroom and in wider school life front and centre. It highlights how strategic leadership, all aspects of school life and classroom practice inform and impact school life for disadvantaged pupils.

THE A–Z OF ADDRESSING DISADVANTAGE

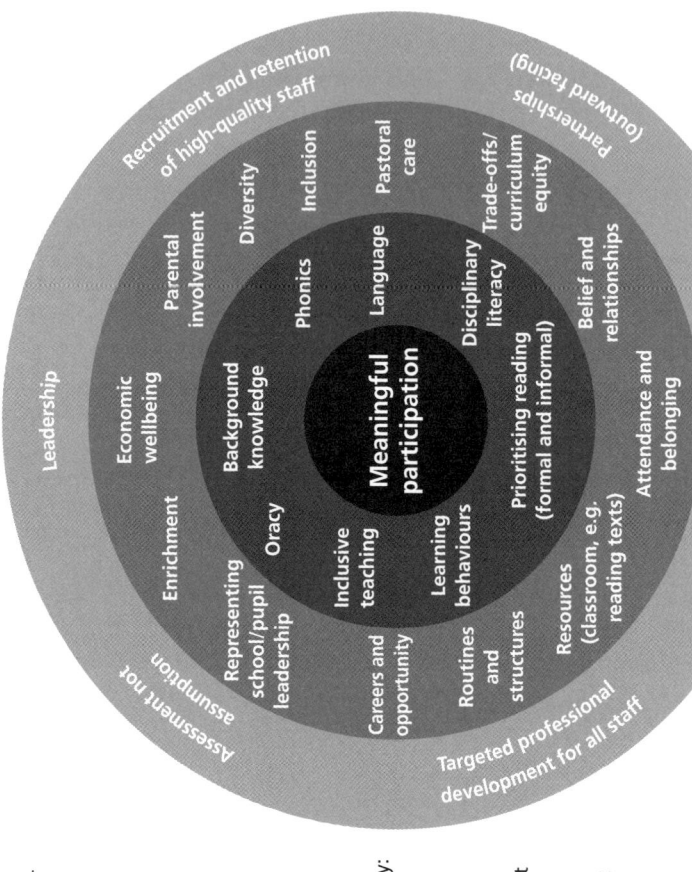

Addressing disadvantage
A benchmarking and reflection resource for developing a whole-school approach to addressing disadvantage, from strategic planning to individual pupils. Helping all to thrive.

Key
- Participation in school life (inside and outside of the classroom). Supported by:
- Classroom priorities, teaching and learning strategies
- Systems, culture, personal development and pastoral care
- Strategic planning/school development
- Golden thread throughout all

Acknowledgements: M. Rowland, V. Flynn, S. Allison, R. Lucas, A. Samways, Y. Thomas

Model C

MODELS

Whichever model is used, it is important to:

- focus on the controllable
- focus on communication and language, and social inclusion
- be specific, especially in working with families
- have clear boundaries (e.g. what is not the role of schools)
- create a team of champions rather than an individual lead
- avoid intervention culture
- focus on short-term and medium-term indicators that show we are on track for achieving long-term goals
- have a strong focus on implementation guidance: engage, unite, reflect.

ASIDE

A CASE STUDY IN MATHEMATICS

Time spent talking with school leaders working in communities with high levels of socio-economic disadvantage is a professional privilege of our work. Recent discussions found us attempting to unpack some of the drivers of the attainment gap in mathematics at the end of Key Stage 2.

The links between language and literacy, and disadvantage are well documented and understood. But issues around numeracy and disadvantage tend to be less well considered. Some of the themes arising from discussions with leaders included in-school matters such as:

- issues relating to working memory – the work of, and classroom guide from, Gathercole and Alloway is helpful here, especially if pupils are anxious or experiencing issues beyond the classroom
- the significant issue of place value, which if not understood in the early years can create problems in later key stages ... and a 'crammed curriculum' can limit time to really check for sound understanding and adapt teaching accordingly

- approaches to early reading such as phonics, which tend to be very clearly codified and supported with excellent resources and training. There tends to be less codification and clarity around early numeracy and this can manifest as teachers and support staff may feel more confident around language and literacy development than they do around mathematics
- ineffective strategic deployment of teaching assistants can create a separation effect if children with the greatest need spend more time away from the teacher. We cannot expect these pupils to be confident with maths if they are not working with qualified teachers, but their peers are.

Looking beyond the school, colleagues shared reflections from their contexts which included influences such as:

- a lack of confidence around numbers and maths at home and within the family may be an issue – parents may lack confidence with maths and as a result talk negatively about the subject influencing motivation and confidence ("I was never any good at maths ….")
- a lack of exposure to early childhood songs and nursery rhymes with patterns and repetition ('five little ducks went swimming one day' and 'one two three four five, once I caught a fish alive'...) may also be influencing familiarity with numbers; added to this, 'counting board games' such as snakes and ladders can be seen to have fallen out of fashion too
- a lack of exposure to concrete or practical applications when it comes to numeracy away from school – growing up in poverty is likely to impact on conversations about money, making children more likely to be negative and associate numbers and maths with stress, anxiety and worry
- issues around oral language development, limited exposure to 'language rich' environments where conversations encourage analysis and problem solving, as well as the challenges associated with reading comprehension.

Discussions explored how issues of lower self-esteem and self-confidence may be drivers that negatively impact on pupils' sense of agency when it comes to maths. These can themselves be exacerbated by overly focusing on a 'catch-up' model of intervention. This can start quite early and be problematic. It can mean that the least confident pupils are working with adults who have lower levels of subject knowledge than the class teacher. Such 'catch-up' interventions appear to be is less effective than academic and social inclusion in the early years and key stage one.

Starting points recognised to be supporting a closing of the gap included:

- ensuring that lower-prior attaining pupils are working with high-quality, well trained, experienced, knowledgeable teachers
- a culture where children from low-income households are held in high regard by all adults in the school
- as professionals, we need to be the champions for pupils whose parents and families might struggle to support learning outside of school or be less confident about how to engage with school life, formal learning, and numeracy
- that it can be powerful, when working with families, to support confidence with numbers, encouraging them to play games and talk positively about numeracy
- we should not rely on what children are doing outside of school as the key to addressing the challenge – parents can help, of course, but it is what we do ourselves in school that really matters.

Numeracy is vital to social, academic and career success, but we need to remember that schools are where professionals are trained to be experts in the teaching of numeracy. However, 'training is taking place' does not always mean that it is enacted effectively in the classroom. We must be minded that the greater the variability in the quality of the mathematics teaching children from disadvantaged backgrounds experience, the greater the likely impact on their learning and outcomes.

The EEF guidance report for Early Years and Key Stage One Mathematics provides us with some helpful steers. Much of the guidance might seem familiar, however it is important to do these things well. Recommendations in the guidance include:

- develop practitioners understanding of how children learn mathematics
- dedicate time for this learning explicitly as a subject and weave through the school day
- use concrete manipulatives to develop understanding as these are fundamental for all children but particularly those that again lack such opportunities outside of school
- ensure that teaching builds on what children already know.

We are reminded that a rigorous approach to checking for understanding is fundamental. Resisting the urge to rush through content and rely on responses from a small number of pupils is particularly important in successful teaching of early maths.

The tyranny of pace is one of the great challenges around mathematics. If children develop low confidence, they will find a way to 'get through' their mathematics lessons rather than really participating and thinking hard. This can result in superficial success at best, rather than thinking hard and experiencing meaningful success.

We need to be relentlessly focused on quality learning experiences for all, securing time for mathematics. We must ensure that children do not find ways of getting through their mathematics, but rather they spend time developing a language of success, and confidence with number.

It is vital that we do not give secret signals to children that only correct answers are valued, and that we instead focus on the process of learning, champion problem solving and model resilience rather than simply valuing the outcome.

The attainment gap in mathematics can be addressed by codifying our approach, being systematic and having the same high expectations and focus that we have for early reading.

With thanks to Rowena Lucas, Hub Lead, Ramsbury English Hub for her advice on this article.

NEEDS

It is important to understand that pupils are not at risk of underachievement because they are PP/SEND or any other label they may be given. They are at risk of underachievement because of the impact of socioeconomic disadvantage on their learning, wellbeing and personal development. A special educational need may also impact on this, exacerbating challenges. But we want to argue that a label-led approach can be problematic. The fact that a pupil is eligible for the PP, or the fact that a pupil has SEND, tells us very little about that pupil as an individual.

The fact that some pupils that did not reach age-related expectations in reading, writing or maths were PP and SEND does not provide useful information for teachers and leaders in planning and implementing strategies to help pupils to thrive. There may be a correlation between the labels and underachievement, but this should not limit our expectations of what children can achieve. The correlation provides limited information about how we respond to the needs of pupils as individuals.

The key messages here:

- The practitioner is the intervention. We need to ensure that staff have the support, expertise, knowledge and agency to help their learners. Consistent, high-quality members of staff are critically important.
- Every pupil is an individual. A focus on labels can disempower teachers and anonymise pupils.
- Pupils with additional needs should get at least equitable access to well-trained, highly qualified staff in comparison to their peers.

Every pupil, irrespective of starting point and background, should be given the chance to thrive. The following list provides some ways in which this may be achieved by a school.

- Ensure that all staff believe that all pupils can make the necessary progress to attain well. There needs to be a collective responsibility for all pupils and families across the school community.
- An understanding that adults in school are often the variable and that children and families need us to be consistent: personnel, routines, interactions and expectations.
- Children and their families must be socially included, and feel that they belong, whether in the classroom, during unstructured times, in sports teams, when there are opportunities to represent the school or be on a student leadership team, or as part of extracurricular activities, residentials and visits. Families should always feel that they are being listened to and not judged.
- There is a meaningful understanding of the impact of low family income on learning and wider school life. Low family income can limit opportunity. It doesn't mean that pupils lack the potential, talent or ability to thrive.
- We must carefully assess issues that are impacting on pupils' learning and opportunity. We can start with issues such as:
  - family income
  - the particular type of special educational need – for example, attention deficit hyperactivity disorder (ADHD)/autism spectrum condition (ASC)/speech, language and communication needs (SLCN)/physical disability/SEMH
  - other factors, including family education levels or support from external agencies.
- We should consider how these issues impact on pupils as individuals. Assessment not assumption. These might include:
  - food insecurity
  - housing/fuel insecurity
  - transport difficulties

- social isolation
- fewer opportunities outside of school
- family/carer short-termism as a result of a crisis cycle
- lack of social networks limiting access to cultural capital, wider aspects of personal development and opportunities, for example work experience, travel, clubs and activities
- difficulties with the cost of school life (even very low cost items or activities)
- societal challenges – uncertain income and unemployment risks; particular judgements, beliefs and assumptions
- negative feelings of self-worth, anxiety and its impact on future agency and aspiration.

- Once needs are identified and understood, we carefully consider how we support individuals:
  - In the classroom, through inclusive teaching strategies, working with high-quality practitioners.
  - By levelling the playing field: frontloading the teaching of knowledge, avoiding the presumption of language and background knowledge, and celebrating the process of learning as well as the outcome.
  - Through targeted academic support (that supplements, not supplants). Be wary of interventions where pupils miss teacher explanation/modelling. And be wary of the disruption of pupils missing 'something different every week'. This can be well intentioned but problematic.
  - Consider the trade-offs (academic and social) if pupils are to be removed from class. Careful provision mapping is needed to avoid over-intervention. The quality of staff leading any interventions should be excellent.
  - Any out-of-school learning is a helpful benefit but should not be essential to progress and attainment.

- Strategies should be rooted in early intervention, improving pupils as learners through:
  - improving self-regulation skills
  - improving communication and language
  - building specific, meaningful vocabulary together as a class team (not reliant on vocabulary lists from the internet)
  - improving reading comprehension
  - ensuring pupils receive meaningful feedback that they can act on
  - meaningful checking for understanding and responsive teaching
  - exceptionally high-quality pastoral care (including supporting good attendance); many pupils face multiple challenges before they even arrive at school
  - an excellent personal-development curriculum; pupils should have meaningful interactions with their peers and build strong friendships
  - ensuring that pupils are able to participate in extracurricular opportunities, enrichment, residentials and wider opportunities to build social stories – the joyful, emotional memories of school life that everyone should experience.
- That we are careful about implementation, avoiding trying to do too many things at once, stuck in a cycle of 'interventions' that impact on pupils academically and socially. As a team, as schools, as a group of schools, we need to Engage, Unite, Reflect, in line with the latest guidance on implementation.
- There should be a dispassionate impact evaluation, focused on the impact on pupils as learners. A robust process-and-impact evaluation framework should be adopted at the start of support – so teachers and leaders can accurately assess its effectiveness. Changes and adaptations can then be made to the practice and strategy where necessary.

HOW CAN WE THINK ABOUT PUPILS WHO ARE DISADVANTAGED WHO ALSO HAVE A SEND DIAGNOSIS?

By talking about 'Pupil Premium Grant pupils' ('PPG pupils'), we have changed our social reality. There is now such a thing as a 'PPG pupil'. This is ripe territory for unconscious bias. By asking the question, 'How do we best support our PPG SEND pupils?', we've created another reality in which there is a group called 'PPG SEND' roaming our corridors. And we are concerned about their attainment.

SEND does not equal low attaining. Disadvantage does not equal low attaining. Neither of these groups is homogeneous.

School leaders are likely interested in the nature of links between poverty and SEND, to better understand the families under their care. Families who are under multiple stressors, including supporting a child with SEND, are more vulnerable to being pushed into poverty. Some children growing up under the stresses of financial hardship are more vulnerable to developing SEND.

> Children with SEND are more likely to become poor, while children living in poverty are more likely to develop SEND. This group of children face greater barriers than their peers in experiencing a happy and fulfilling education and greater barriers in achieving the qualifications that might create opportunities later in life.
>
> Source: The Joseph Rowntree Foundation (2016)

So, a sensitivity to individual circumstances and difficulties is, of course, key to building productive relationships between home and school. Most practitioners would be doing this anyway, so what should we be 'doing' about 'PPG SEND'?

Families on lower incomes or living in poverty may struggle with time and resources to navigate the SEND system in comparison to more-affluent families. They deserve our care and support.

- **Beware of the thinking trap, i.e. thinking that particular groups have 'barriers'.** All pupils have the capacity to grow and develop but this is severely hindered if teachers stop thinking in terms of 'What do they know? What do they need to know next?'.

- **Don't imagine this as a homogeneous group.** No two pupils are the same, but thinking through labels can give this illusion. Within this group – if it is actually a 'group' – will be pupils of varying strengths and needs. Some children eligible for PP who have SEND diagnoses are exceptionally high attainers.

- **Don't imagine that staff haven't already thought about pupils' needs.** Trying to think about this knotty issue, balancing thinking about societal prejudice and individual pupil need, is overloading for busy school leaders. We can fall into a trap of 'What do I do about PPG SEND? What are their challenges?' and feel rather lost. However, leaders already have a wealth of knowledge collected over time about their pupils, their strengths and needs from: pupil-progress meetings; day-to-day, lesson-to-lesson, moment-to-moment observations; SEND-support meetings; education, health and care plan (EHCP) annual reviews; parent and carer consultations; end-of-year reports. The information is often already there for us.

- **Look at the lived experience of pupils in classrooms.** Practitioners should be aware of systemic prejudice and play their part to disrupt it. However, there is so much mileage in examining the educational experience of pupils within our classrooms. Watch pupils of concern in lessons and consider the learning from their point of view. Can they see the board? Can they hear the teacher and other pupils? Did the teacher ensure the paired talk was accessible, successful and accountable? Has their teacher checked their understanding? Do they need glasses? What is the quality of their interaction with staff – focused around learning and based in an interested, kindly relationship?

The challenges pupils face may be multiple and complex. External support from outside agencies may be needed (and not always readily available). Multiple challenges mean multiple complexities. Where possible, it is vital to avoid an overly complicated response.

Pupils who experience multiple and complex challenges with their learning and personal development may need ambitious, personalised, individual approaches to help them in the short- and medium term to enable them to thrive in the long term. The ambition for every pupil, irrespective of the challenges they face, should be a life rooted in opportunity. The Grange Special School in Manchester is a model of good practice with this.

> **ASIDE**
>
> **CASE STUDY: ADDRESSING DISADVANTAGE AT MANCHESTER COMMUNICATION ACADEMY (MCA)**
>
> September 2024 marks 20 years since my teaching career began. That's 20 exam series and 20 results days. Twenty years of seeing young people open those little envelopes and being overcome with joy and pride.
>
> This year, the lasting memory I will have is of the football team (2024 Manchester Cup Champions) arriving together, hiding behind the drama studio curtains, apprehensive and visibly nervous, to open their little envelopes. I'll remember hearing the sounds of joy when they realised what they had achieved; pride for themselves and for each other. The urgency to call loved ones and to say thank you to teachers. Recalling it now brings back the goosebumps and the lump in my throat.
>
> This moment mattered to those students and it will always matter. Here is an environment where those boys can thrive on the football field, but also academically and personally; this was a collective success for them. My four-year-old daughter was with me as we watched this unfold. She held my hand and said, 'Mummy, they are so happy!'. (Another lump in the throat.)
>
> How lucky we are to witness these moments and be part of their journey.

But this sits within the wider context of what many students from disadvantaged backgrounds are facing. On The Sutton Trust website (www.suttontrust.com/our-priorities/), these statistics can be found as a stark reminder of the reality facing many of these students:

> **20%**
> The proportion of families in the bottom third of the earnings distribution eligible for the existing offer of 30 hours of early education and childcare for three- and four-year-olds.
> —
> A Fair Start?

> Promising primary school pupils from disadvantaged households fall
> **ONE GRADE**
> per subject behind equally talented affluent peers at GCSE.
> —
> Social Mobility: The Next Generation

> **1000**
> The number of young people from under-represented areas that are 'missing' from 30 top universities each year, despite getting the grades.
> —
> 25 Years of University Access

> **5%**
> Fewer degree apprenticeships are eligible for free school meals than those starting undergraduate study.
> —
> The Recent Evolution of Apprenticeships

> People in Britain's top jobs are
> **FIVE TIMES MORE LIKELY**
> to have attended a private school than the general population.
> —
> Elitist Britain, 2019

> This means that disadvantaged young people are
> **4.5 TIMES LESS LIKELY**
> to become a top earner than someone who attended a private school.
> —
> Universities and Social Mobility

So, despite our joy, our outrage continues and with that, our relentless pursuit for better.

At Manchester Communication Academy, our approach to leading a culture where all students, but especially our disadvantaged students, can thrive, can be summarised as follows:

1. **Challenge a deficit narrative.** In 2018, the Education Policy Institute published its annual report on education in England and included an analysis and commentary on the different practices within school that impact on

outcomes for disadvantaged students. One factor that is identified is that of unconscious bias. According to the Office of Diversity and Outreach at University of California, San Francisco, unconscious biases are 'social stereotypes about certain groups of people that individuals form outside their conscious awareness'.

In some schools, teachers and leaders may hold these unconscious biases about students from lower socioeconomic backgrounds. Phrases like 'our kids can't do homework' or 'school isn't valued in this community' all lead to lower expectations and lower aspirations. They are also simply not true. Our community is asset-rich; our children are capable and brilliant. As a leader, it is important to call out any unconscious bias and challenge any deficit narrative. Even better, ensure your school is a place where everyone feels empowered to call it out.

2. **Establish a safe, structured environment, rooted in routines and habits.** Young people thrive when they know what to expect. They can also thrive when they have the cognitive capacity to learn. We can create this learning capacity by removing any distractions or unpredictable situations that require cognitive processes. Once behaviours become routine and habitual, young people can then direct their attention to the important information; the knowledge that is being taught. A consistent approach to simple activities like starts to lessons, movement around the building and responding to questions can provide a safe, stable and predictable environment.

3. **Prioritise teaching and learning alongside exceptional pastoral care and wellbeing.** 'The EEF guide to the Pupil Premium' (2024b (updated)) advises taking a tiered approach to PP spending, ensuring that an investment in high-quality teaching is a top priority. At MCA, high-quality professional development is our number-one priority for our PP strategy. We have invested in a director of professional development and a team of teacher educators to ensure that staff members are equipped with the knowledge and skills to effectively embed evidence-informed practice across the academy.

We also recognise the importance of authentic pastoral care that is rooted in genuine relationships with families. Our family partnership team is dedicated to finding ways to support families through our bespoke early-help framework. Not only does this mean that barriers can be removed early, but there is a dialogue between home and school that is invaluable.

4. **Find valued time and space for a high-quality personal-development curriculum.** At MCA, our school values are Respect, Responsibility and Resilience, and we encourage our students to Be Brave, Be Brilliant and Be Kind. An effective personal-development curriculum is not simply a series of lessons mapped out on a curriculum journey. A personal-development curriculum permeates every corner of an effective school culture. How do teachers interact with young people and with each other? How do you support staff to tackle the difficult conversations with honesty, integrity and kindness? What do you recognise and what do you celebrate? Personal development takes place within and outside the classrooms, where students learn from the models they see.

5. **Be restless.** Finally, we are never done and we never will be. A leader of a culture where children can thrive creates an environment where success is celebrated but so is grit, determination and a belief that any glass ceilings can be smashed.

I'd like to finish this section with a saying from Jonny Bairstow, England cricketer, who we were lucky enough to have join us on our September INSET day. He said: 'Be proud of where you come from, but have pride in where you can get to.'

Schools that encapsulate that will be places where students can thrive, now and in their futures.

Susie Fraser with contributions from Sue Watmough and John Rowlands

ORACY

BREAKING THE SILENCE: HOW ORACY AND SEL UNLOCK POTENTIAL IN DISADVANTAGED LEARNERS

In the fight against poverty and inequality, oracy and social and emotional learning (SEL) are two powerful tools that can level the playing field for disadvantaged pupils. These life skills are essential for empowering young people to overcome the barriers that often accompany socioeconomic challenges. By developing strong communication and social–emotional skills, children are better equipped to succeed academically, build meaningful relationships and unlock greater opportunities for a brighter future.

The power of oracy

Oracy is the ability to effectively use spoken language, encompassing both expressive and receptive skills, to communicate, understand and interpret information. For pupils from disadvantaged backgrounds, strong oracy skills can be transformative. These skills enable children to participate actively in classroom discussions, articulate their thoughts in interviews and presentations, and engage confidently in both academic and professional settings.

For pupils facing economic hardships, the ability to communicate effectively can be a game-changer. It helps them break down barriers, advocate for themselves and access opportunities that might otherwise remain out of reach. By focusing on oracy, educators can help pupils from all backgrounds develop the confidence and clarity needed to navigate complex social and professional environments.

The role of social and emotional learning (SEL)

SEL involves developing the skills to manage emotions, set goals, show empathy for others, establish positive relationships and make responsible decisions. These competencies are especially important for children from low-income families who often experience higher levels of stress due to their circumstances. High stress in children, which correlates with the stress levels of their caregivers, can hinder academic performance and social development.

Through SEL, children learn to manage their emotions and behaviours. This is essential for creating a stable foundation for learning. When pupils feel safe and supported, they are more likely to engage in their education and less likely to be derailed by the challenges they face outside the classroom.

Supporting teachers and building relationships

Teachers play a pivotal role in nurturing oracy and SEL, but they need time and support to build authentic relationships with their pupils. This is especially important at the start of the school year or after long breaks when establishing trust and understanding is critical. Teachers who can create a safe and supportive environment help people feel valued, which in turn boosts their confidence and willingness to participate.

Investing in teacher development is essential for this process. Educators need the tools and training to integrate oracy and SEL into their daily routines effectively. By establishing clear norms and providing consistent support, teachers can help pupils develop the communication and emotional skills they need to succeed.

THE INTERSECTION OF ORACY AND SEL

Oracy and SEL are deeply interconnected. Language is inherently social and develops through interaction, making it a vital component of SEL. Through conversations, children learn to navigate emotions, build empathy and solve problems. These skills are not only essential for academic success but also for life beyond the classroom.

Oracy helps children find their voice and express their identity, while SEL deepens their self-awareness and understanding of both themselves and others. Together, these skills empower them to use their voice in constructive, meaningful and impactful ways that enhance their wellbeing and contribute to the greater good. This powerful combination lays the foundation for young people to achieve equity and excellence, regardless of their socioeconomic background.

CONCLUSION

Oracy and SEL are more than just educational tools; they are essential life skills for overcoming the challenges of poverty and inequality. These skills are also key to enhancing pupils' overall wellbeing, helping them to manage stress, build resilience and develop a positive sense of self. By equipping pupils with strong communication and emotional skills, we empower them to overcome obstacles, seize opportunities and maintain their mental and emotional health. Supporting teachers in this mission is critical, as they are the ones who can create the nurturing environments where these skills and wellbeing can flourish. In focusing on oracy, SEL and wellbeing, we take a significant step toward creating a more equitable and just society for all.

ASIDE

CASE STUDY: 'TALK AND TOAST' AT BEDGROVE INFANT SCHOOL, BUCKINGHAMSHIRE

Here at Bedgrove Infant School, 'disadvantage' is not a label that we use to group or define pupils. We look at each pupil individually and consider their experiences and their opportunities. Pupils' experiences can either remain consistent or significantly change in a single moment, so it is important that we intervene early and the support each pupil needs remains a non-negotiable. We have devised a group intervention called 'Talk and Toast' which continues to grow and develop over time.

'Talk and Toast' is an ever-changing intervention that is linked directly to the current needs of our pupils. The premise of 'Talk and Toast' is as simple as it sounds if the following fundamentals happen:

1. It is a non-negotiable (it happens daily, no matter what the circumstance).
2. The logistics and preparation are key.
3. The adult is the intervention. The adult is at the heart of each session so they need relevant training, a caring nature, an understanding of each individual pupil's needs and to be a consistent, trusted adult.
4. Pupils are selected based on evidence compiled from staff members (observations, knowledge of home/family life and data).

Through 'Talk and Toast', we celebrate pupils' successes, we provide a space for pupils to belong, we expose them to new experiences and we support their acquisition of language.

While we know it is important to identify those pupils who may not have the quality of opportunities, labelling children as 'disadvantaged' runs a high risk of anonymising them based on assumption. By not using this label, we are able to control the narrative in our setting.

Louise Sim and Ellice Camfield-Grant

PRESUMPTION

THE 'THREE Ps'

Presume at your peril! At all costs, you must avoid the 'Three Ps', i.e. the following three 'presumptions':

- **Presumption of background knowledge**: Do pupils have the knowledge to participate in their lessons?
- **Presumption of language and oracy**: Can pupils access the language being used? Are they getting opportunities to talk? Are they being heard?
- **Presumption of good learning behaviours**: Do we explicitly ensure that pupils are actively participating in their learning in a group setting, or independently? Do pupils understand the process of learning?

Presumption of background knowledge

Pupils in a Year 7 history lesson will bring a wide range of prior knowledge on the Black Death. Some will have talked about this with their parents, maybe watched a documentary about it or even read about it in a book. As a result, they will have a relatively well-developed schema on the topic, and so grafting further knowledge about the Black Death onto this existing knowledge will make this new learning easier.

Other pupils will have done none of these things, so will have a very limited background knowledge on the topic, making learning considerably more difficult. A consequence of this is that those better-informed pupils will dominate the discourse in the lesson, while the others sit quietly in the corner, wondering 'how do they know that?'.

We need to demystify and unpackage this for these students, so that they understand how their peers have acquired this knowledge.

The point is, we can't presume the level of background knowledge that they have, so we need to empower all pupils by making sure they have the knowledge required to be successful. So, take some time at the start of a lesson/task to discuss and share the knowledge that pupils will need to be able to tackle what they are going to do. If we don't do this, we'll be putting some pupils at a disadvantage (with thanks to Shaun Allison).

> **Example:**
>
> Pupils are told they are studying *Romeo and Juliet*.
>
> Pupil A has been to Verona. They stood on Juliet's balcony. They have seen the ballet at the Royal Opera House and have watched the film. Their parents studied (and enjoyed) the play at school. Pupil A recently saw a modern retelling of the play at Regent's Park Open Air Theatre. They are really motivated when told about the play. They are keen to answer questions from the teacher when exploring prior knowledge.
>
> Pupil B is not sure whether Verona is a real place, but knows a few quotes and a rough outline of the story. They keep quiet to avoid getting it wrong. They present as passive and disengaged. They think Pupil A is 'magically clever', as opposed to acquiring the knowledge through opportunity.
>
> This is how disadvantage can present in the classroom. How we level the playing field through frontloading, and activating prior knowledge in an inclusive way, is fundamental to success for disadvantaged pupils.

Presumption of language and oracy

The language gap is the attainment gap. If pupils are poor readers and have poor vocabulary, accessing the curriculum is going to present a significant challenge for them. So rather than presuming that pupils have a firm grasp of the tier 2 and 3 vocabulary we use in lessons, we need to employ a range of strategies to support them with this. For example:

- **Incidental teaching of vocabulary** – when reading rich texts in class and using tier 2 and 3 vocabulary, stop and discuss words and their meaning.
- **Explicit vocabulary instruction** – plan what tier 2 and 3 vocabulary will be used in a topic and explicitly teach this vocabulary beforehand.
- **Word consciousness** – teach the common root words to help pupils decode other words when they meet them.

Presumption of good learning behaviours

Going back to the example above, when our more advantaged pupils share their prior knowledge of a topic, it's important for them to share how their learning behaviours have enabled them to acquire that knowledge. Ask them, 'How do you know that?'. This is important because it shows other pupils that their peers don't just know this by magic! They know it because they read, listen and are inquisitive about the world around them. They are articulating their learning behaviours.

A learning behaviour can be thought of as a behaviour that is necessary in order for a person to learn effectively in the group setting of the classroom (Ellis and Tod, 2018). These behaviours can be grouped into emotional, social and cognitive learning behaviours.

A pupil's background will clearly influence these behaviours, so we need to be conscious of this and think about how we will support pupils with this. For example, the ability to self-regulate your learning is a key characteristic of an effective learner, however, this will be a struggle for some pupils. To support pupils, we need to model how we plan, monitor and evaluate our learning when we are approaching a new task. We can't presume that they will be confident with this.

ASIDE

CASE STUDY: ADDRESSING DISADVANTAGE AT DURRINGTON HIGH SCHOOL, WEST SUSSEX

Tackling disadvantage at Durrington threads through everything we do. All day and every day. If I had to summarise our approach, I would say that it is based around the following six points.

1. **Breaking the link between family income and academic attainment is our moral purpose.** As school leaders, it's easy for us to pat ourselves on the back when things are going well – when attainment is high among groups of pupils or in particular subjects. However, we need to be more honest with ourselves. If our disadvantaged pupils are underachieving, it doesn't matter how well everyone else is doing; we need to do better. This is the most stubborn challenge facing school leaders – but it's one we can't ignore.

2. **Having the highest expectations.** We need to believe in our students and instil in them a belief that they can achieve amazing things. Most pupils, irrespective of their backgrounds, have high aspirations. That is not the issue. The issue is they see too many barriers in their way to achieving these aspirations. Our job is to help them break through these barriers. For many (not all) of these students, we will be the only adults in their lives who have the highest expectations of them. We never dumb these down. We have the highest expectations of how they write, how they speak, how they present themselves, how they behave, etc.

3. **All pupils, irrespective of their background, need to feel included in school and successful.** All pupils need to feel a sense of belonging in school. They need to feel that their thoughts and opinions are valued in lessons; that they can make a great contribution to extracurricular clubs; that school trips are for them; that adults in the school are pleased to see

them; that their efforts and endeavours, in and out of lessons, are valued and celebrated. They need to know that they matter. This is at the heart of improving attendance; we need to show them that when they attend school, it makes school a better place.

4. **The most effective strategies for tackling educational disadvantage focus on improving the pupil as a learner**. For us, this is really important. Our teaching needs to shape pupils as learners – and this is especially important for our disadvantaged learners. So what does this mean?

   - We need to help them develop as readers. If they can't read well, they won't be able to access the curriculum. So, this is a priority.
   - We need to use explicit and implicit vocabulary instruction strategies to build their tier 2 and 3 vocabulary. If they haven't read much, their vocabulary will be poor. So, we have to teach it explicitly.
   - We need to teach metacognitive strategies explicitly to our pupils, so they can become effective, self-regulated learners.
   - We need to shape our curriculum and teaching so that it supports (and fills gaps in) background knowledge. Don't presume background knowledge; build it deliberately.

5. **We must all be experts in the pupils we are teaching and use this to shape our teaching**. If we are to achieve number 3, we need to know our pupils really well. What are their strengths as learners? What are their challenges? How can we support them to overcome these challenges? A really important part of this is guarding against assumption. We cannot assume that all disadvantaged pupils have the same challenges to learning. They won't have. We need to invest time in finding out what the challenges are for individual pupils and then framing our teaching around this. So for us, relationships are key; they are key to understanding the challenges to learning that our pupils will have and then working with them to address these challenges.

6. **We need to see life through the lens of a disadvantaged pupil.** Every decision we make as a leader needs to be seen through the lens of a disadvantaged learner. The trips that we offer – are they out of reach for some? Extracurricular challenges that we set – will they have someone to support them with this? The homework we set – have they got a quiet place where they can do it? Many of our students live complex and demanding lives. We need to understand this and give them the necessary support to ensure that this doesn't exclude them from school.

Shaun Allison

QUIBBLES

Intervening to symptoms can lead to generalised assumptions. For example, a lack of participation in clubs or inconsistent attendance can be mistaken for a lack of motivation, interest or aspiration. In reality, there are likely to be much more complex drivers sitting behind these issues. Generalised assumptions can inadvertently lead to bias and a deficit discourse around disadvantaged pupils.

Rather, it is important to get under the surface of how low family income is impacting on learning. Furthermore, focus on those things that are most in the school's control. For example, we have more control and influence over pupils' oral language than we do over their housing situation.

The table below should support school leaders in steering towards underlying causes, rather than focusing on symptoms or assumptions. Symptom-led approaches are likely to lead to tightly focused activity that helps pupils to be more successful academically, personally and socially. This can only come from precise focus on the underlying causes.

THE A–Z OF ADDRESSING DISADVANTAGE

Symptoms	Potential causes	Assumptions/actions to be wary of
Limited progress in individual subjects/across the board Low end-of-key-stage attainment Poor/inconsistent attendance Non-attendance at clubs, enrichment, etc. Limited participation in student leadership Non-completion of homework	• Physical- and mental-health issues • Oral language • Language comprehension • Opportunity beyond school (enrichment, homework, building social capital) • Lack of affordability • Lack of belonging/confidence/inclusion • Inconsistent teaching and learning • Recruitment and retention issues (teachers and support staff) • Mobility • Social challenges beyond school • Housing issues • Family education levels • Motivation and confidence • Over-intervention • Social isolation • Geographical issues	• Disadvantaged pupils/families don't value education • Disadvantaged pupils have poor behaviour • Disadvantaged pupils are only interested/motivated in particular subjects • Disadvantaged pupils/families have low aspirations • That poverty is static • That pupils/families are in some way to be blamed for being poor • Lowering expectations/support based on parental behaviours • Blanket approaches: 'PP first' • A lack of engagement with education is due to poverty • Generalising • Unintentionally isolating

ASIDE

CASE STUDY: LEADING A CULTURE WHERE DISADVANTAGED STUDENTS CAN THRIVE AT STRIVE4 ACADEMY TRUST, REDBRIDGE

This is highly nuanced and hard to capture. The vast majority of what we do is not actually focusing on disadvantaged pupils; it's focusing on 'the pupil', all-encompassing. We are uncomfortable defining a pupil as 'disadvantaged' or as a 'pupil with a disadvantage in their learning', not just because it separates them – and even in schools where the ethos and culture are incredibly strong, the use of such labels will trigger unconscious bias – but also because there are so many learners who have hidden disadvantages and potential barriers.

No matter how much we seek to know the pupil, some remain hidden. We know that success is the result of a number of factors including emotional awareness, resilience, self-advocacy and knowledge. All of our staff understand that this multi-faceted nature of success is key, not only to securing a pupil's success but also in securing their own. The more that staff feel success and see success, the more the pupils will. Strategically, we focus on staff first, despite us being a child-first organisation. Our focus is very much on securing excellent teaching, and that teaching is nestled within a nurturing and inclusive environment. So, simplistically, our approaches fall within three domains:

- pupils feel ready to learn
- pupils are supported to learn
- pupils actually learn.

Some examples as a flavour:

Pupils feel ready to learn
Our approach here is to have a strong, all-embracing culture wherein everyone feels safe and valued. This is reflected in the aesthetics of the school, school

policies, procedures, staffing structure, recruitment and open partnerships with families and external agencies. We have the usual approaches for making sure parents are listened to and that they have a genuine voice (workshops, watch a lesson, come in and read, class talks, 'Connect' sessions, coffee with the head etc.) but staff have a particular day-in-day-out focus on making connections with the parents of those pupils whose families appear a little distanced from the school. This is policy. We also have a smiling policy – which seems ridiculous – and ensure that all staff are in the playground each morning with targeted parents to smile at, engage with or share a positive moment with. Much of our CPD focuses on empathetic relationships.

Pupils are supported to learn

The approach here is a nuanced and tiered pastoral support programme for the most vulnerable pupils that is in addition to a strong ethos and culture across the organisation. This works synchronously with a similarly tiered academic 'intervention' programme.

Through an 'agile', tiered, in-school approach to pastoral and academic support, the individual needs and wider context of our most vulnerable pupils are assessed and tailored support is put in place. What we mean by agile is that our approach is constantly changing and adapting to the changing needs of the community. Of course, the nature of this support is wide ranging from counselling, play therapy, pre-teaching, in-class coaching of pupils, tutoring and simply touching base to remind a pupil that they are in our thoughts and are cared for. What makes this work is that a large proportion of the tier 5 support is undertaken by the class teachers working closely with the pupil in the classroom, forming those relationships necessary for them to feel safe and cared for. Tiers 4–1 become progressively more specialist, although not requiring, at this point, external intervention. It is a whole-school, shared responsibility requiring staff to know their pupils inside out but, even more importantly, to know how to use that knowledge for the greatest impact.

Pupils actually learn

Teaching has to lead to learning for all, not just the 75%. One approach is to invest heavily in integrated CPD – and the right CPD – for *all* staff. This takes many forms from in-class partnership teaching, coaching, lesson study, in-the-moment feedback, working parties, as well as bespoke training. Our focus is on developing the expertise and self-efficacy of all staff, leading to research-informed, consistent, inclusive, pedagogical practice and a shared expectation of striving for excellence, both in and out of the classroom. Every moment is a learning moment.

At the same time, we retain quality, committed staff and so giving long-term consistency for learners. While this could be perceived as being a staff-centric approach, it is the opposite. Our staff know what effective teaching is and understand that poor or naïve teaching habits hinder learning.

Amanda Jennings

RESEARCH

Research evidence should be used to inform decision-making. It should be used to challenge assumptions and beliefs, not simply to justify decisions already taken.

Research evidence should not be used to tell teachers and leaders exactly what to do; each pupil and each classroom is far too complex and unique. But research can inform our decision-making when planning our strategies for tackling educational disadvantage. It can suggest 'best bets' and also where to be cautious. In summary:

- Evidence should inform our decision-making.
- Evidence should be used to challenge our views, not just confirm them.
- Beware of confirmation bias and publication bias.

Research evidence with the right school culture, values, professional judgement, consideration of the needs of pupils and families, and teacher agency is most likely to be helpful.

ASIDE

CASE STUDY: HOW EVIDENCE CAN HELP SCHOOLS WITH DECISION MAKING, CORNWALL RESEARCH SCHOOL

As Professor Becky Francis, Chief Executive of the EEF, has said, 'Our leaders are more evidence-rich than a decade ago. But leaders face a clear choice about the ways in which they use it. Ironically, as the language of evidence proliferates, there is a risk that it loses its impact. Surface-level compliance is the biggest threat to any change in education.'

Those of us in the Research Schools Network used to ask schools, 'If you are not using evidence, what are you using?'. But as the new EEF guidance report on implementation (2024a) suggests, evidence use has proliferated throughout the system.

> A culture shift is occurring in English schools towards widespread engagement with research, with evidence-based resources becoming go-to sources of guidance. Yet awareness of evidence does not necessarily result in improved outcomes: implementation is critical for turning engagement with research into tangible changes in school practices and pupil outcomes, including, crucially, for pupils experiencing socioeconomic disadvantage.
>
> Most robust evaluations of education interventions show little or no impact on pupil outcomes compared to existing practices. Making evidence-informed decisions on what to implement in the first place is therefore vital.

Schools can enhance their decision-making processes significantly by systematically integrating research evidence into their practices. The use of evidence in education ensures that decisions are informed by the best available knowledge, leading to improved outcomes for students.

Alongside the cross-cutting behaviours that drive effective implementation and the contextual factors that influence implementation described in the new EEF guidance report 'A school's guide to implementation' (2024a), schools should look to use a structured process. By adopting a practical and tailored set of implementation strategies organised into manageable phases – Explore, Prepare, Deliver and Sustain – schools can apply the behaviours and contextual factors to their day-to-day work.

An important starting point would be for schools to diagnose and identify the priorities and needs for their context precisely and accurately. Without accurate diagnosis, any strategy, intervention or practice change may not address the

RESEARCH

root cause of the problem. This, in turn, could lead to wasted time, effort and resources in the push for improving outcomes for students.

When I was 10 years old, I fell ill. My symptoms were headaches, nausea, stiffness and fever. My mother took me to the doctor who told her I had a flu-like virus and that bed rest and fluids should see me right. My symptoms persisted and my mother, being worried, took me back to the doctor. The diagnosis and suggested treatment remained the same. With her intuition as a mother, she took me back a third and even fourth time, insisting that I was really ill, until finally a second doctor diagnosed me with meningitis. I was rushed to the hospital where I stayed for a week, was given antibiotics (it was bacterial meningitis) and, after a range of drips, tests (including several, painful lumbar punctures) and treatment, I recovered and was sent home. *My point is this: correct diagnosis of need can help inform us of the correct treatment, leading to the desired outcome.*

After assessing the needs and context of their setting carefully, schools should also consider assessing their approach. What does the research evidence say about interventions that match their needs and priorities? How might such approaches be implemented?

Schools need access to high-quality, relevant research to inform their decisions. This can be facilitated by subscribing to educational research journals, utilising online databases and engaging with organisations like the Research Schools Network or the EEF that synthesise research into accessible formats. The EEF's Teaching and Learning Toolkit, for instance, provides summaries of the effectiveness of various educational interventions, allowing schools to make informed choices.

Schools can also foster a culture of evidence use in decision-making. Creating a culture that values evidence is the foundation for effective decision-making. School leaders should champion the use of evidence and model this behaviour. This might involve encouraging teachers and staff to engage with research, providing time and resources for professional development, and fostering an environment where questioning and reflective practice are the norms.

Celebrating successes and sharing stories of how evidence-based interventions have led to positive outcomes can further reinforce this culture.

Building the capacity of staff to understand and use research is critical. Effective professional development opportunities can focus on how to interpret and apply research findings. Workshops, training sessions and collaborative-learning groups can help staff become more research literate. Schools can also appoint evidence champions or create research leads who can guide their colleagues in integrating evidence into their teaching practices.

When implementing an intervention, schools must also monitor and evaluate its impact. This involves setting clear, measurable objectives and using data to assess whether these objectives are being met. Considering and planning to monitor implementation outcomes will help schools keep track of how well the implementation process is going, increasing the likelihood of the final outcomes of improving student outcomes being successful. This cycle of continuous improvement and reflective behaviour ensures that practices are improved, refined and optimised over time.

Schools can benefit from participating in networks and partnerships that promote the sharing of evidence and best practice. Collaborating with other schools, local authorities and educational researchers can provide new insights and help schools stay updated on the latest research. Such networks also offer opportunities for peer learning and support, which can enhance the overall capacity for evidence use.

Integrating evidence into school decision-making processes can lead to more effective teaching and improved student outcomes. By fostering a culture of evidence use, accessing high-quality research, developing staff capacity, implementing and evaluating interventions, engaging in collaborative networks, and following implementation guidance, schools can ensure that their practices are grounded in the best-available evidence. This strategic approach not only enhances decision-making, but also contributes to a more informed, reflective and, ultimately, successful educational system.

John Rodgers

STRATEGY

Developing your PP strategy should be a team effort. Adopting the 'Engage, Unite, Reflect' approach set out in the implementation section provides a better chance of success. A high-quality plan on paper is only beneficial to pupils if it can be enacted effectively.

- Does the intent statement reflect your approach and ambitions for your disadvantaged pupils?
- Do the challenges reflect your priorities for your disadvantaged pupils? Are they actionable/in the school's gift? Is there a collective understanding/response for addressing them?
- Are the intended outcomes and success criteria actually outcomes (as opposed to activities)? Do they link to the challenges? Are they measurable?
- Is the activity linked to challenges and underpinned by evidence? Is it manageable? Should anything be taken out of the strategy?
- Who are your key staff for implementation? Do staff understand their role in the implementation process?
- Are there any possible problems with implementation?

A MODEL OF EXCELLENCE

Greenshaw High School in Sutton is a model of excellence, from strategy planning to the classroom. Phil Stock, Deputy Headteacher, describes some of the work done by the school here: https://researchschool.org.uk/greenshaw/news/making-the-difference. Phil's work is both inspirational and purposeful.

The school's published PP strategy is a model of good practice. It reflects all that was observed during the review. There is a strong focus on the classroom, underpinned by research evidence and there is a collective responsibility for the approach.

The front page sets out some basic administrative information.

The intent statement sets out the school's ambitions for disadvantaged pupils, and how they will be achieved.

The school's approach is very strong. It is leading to impressive outcomes for disadvantaged pupils. The focus on reading develops pupils' vistas and background knowledge, and improves them as learners.

The challenges are rooted in assessment and observation, with rigorous thought and time included to give a rich picture of how disadvantage impacts on learning, and where provision needs to be even better.

The intended outcomes link closely to the challenges, and rightly include a range of short-, medium- and long-term outcomes, using qualitative and quantitative measures.

The activity in the plan is evidence-rich, and the evidence that underpins the activity has been given detailed consideration. The engagement with evidence to support activity is excellent.

The evaluation model is clearly set out and carried out in a dispassionate way. The evaluation is about improving, not proving. Again, it is a model of good practice. The full strategy can be found here: https://www.greenshawlearningtrust.co.uk/attachments/download.asp?file=2381&type=pdf.

These are key questions for leaders and governors in identifying and overcoming the barriers to learning and development:

- What is our priority for getting it right for disadvantaged pupils in the classroom?
- Does this link to our identified challenges?
- What is *not* a priority (even though it may be important!)?
- Do all staff understand low family income and its impact?
- Do all staff and governors understand their role in the school's strategy?

- Are intended outcomes and success criteria clear?
- Have issues with implementation been considered from the start (from the perspective of all staff)?

Understanding challenges in your strategy:

- Are the challenges rooted in recent assessments and observations?
- Are they drawing on a range of sources?
- Are they reflective of teacher experiences?
- Do they include academic development, personal development and pastoral issues?
- Are issues such as quality of teaching and consistency of leadership acknowledged?
- Are challenges underlying causes or symptoms?

HOW SHOULD WE RESPOND TO DISADVANTAGE AND ENSURE THE INCLUSION OF PUPILS?

Focus on giving teachers and support staff the expertise, training, knowledge and support to help pupils to thrive. Approaches should always align with **assessment of need**.

The DfE guidance on PP (2024) states:

> When diagnosing the needs of your disadvantaged pupils, you should bear in mind that you do not have to spend your Pupil Premium so that it solely benefits eligible pupils. You can use it to support other pupils with identified needs, for example, those who have or have had a social worker or are a carer. You can also use it on whole-class approaches, for example, high-quality teaching, which will also benefit all pupils.

Every pupil is different so they may need help in any of the following common priority areas:

- oral language development
- phonics
- reading for purpose and pleasure

- vocabulary support and acquisition
- language comprehension
- contextual subject knowledge/cultural capital gaps
- gaps in prior learning/targeted academic support
- behaviour for learning
- social and emotional health/mental health
- self-confidence/agency
- lack of enrichment opportunities outside of school
- social isolation
- targeted pastoral care (including attendance)
- personal development – PSHE (personal, social, health (and economic) education), work experience
- consistency of routines, structures and expectations.

As set out earlier on pages 104-5, outside of the classroom, low family income may present as one or more of the following:

- food insecurity
- housing/fuel insecurity
- transport difficulties
- social isolation
- few opportunities outside of school
- family/carer short-termism as a result of a crisis cycle
- lack of social networks limiting access to cultural capital, wider aspects of personal development and opportunities, for example, work experience, travel, clubs and activities
- difficulties with the cost of school life (even very low cost items or activities)
- societal challenges – uncertain income and unemployment risks
- particular judgements, beliefs and assumptions
- negative feelings of self-worth, anxiety and the impact of these feelings on future agency and aspiration.

Personal development

High-quality enrichment opportunities may have a disproportionate impact on pupils from low-income families, who may lack opportunity outside of school. Many schools report that pupils from low-income families are less likely to participate. It is important to ensure pupils feel included and that families are supported with economic wellbeing.

School leaders should be intentional about disadvantaged pupils being included in student leadership opportunities and playing prominent roles representing the school in sports, music and community work. Positive experiences at school lead to motivation and belonging.

Careers education should start early and be of high quality, broadening vistas and building social capital. The quality of careers education (especially work experience) should never be limited to personal connections. This widens the disadvantage gap.

Good enrichment

Enrichment can be defined as any activity that creates opportunity, broadens horizons, builds confidence and promotes social inclusion and belonging.

It is especially important for pupils that lack opportunities beyond school, but should not isolate or be only open to particular pupils. Quality opportunity should be available to all.

Enrichment supports pupils to feel as though they are contributing to their own personal development, but it also helps them to feel that they are contributors to the school community. It is not simply about getting more disadvantaged pupils into clubs.

Pastoral care

High-quality pastoral care is not an optional extra. It is fundamental to success.

Language and communication are at the heart of relationships, friendships and wellbeing. Emotional wellbeing and language and communication go hand in hand. This includes supporting families with:

- social and emotional/mental health, such as by offering counselling

- physical health, such as food and other life essentials
- family support, including working with external agencies.

As with academic learning, it is important that assessment, not assumption, drives any strategic approach and that practices are high quality and rooted in evidence.

The 'Pupil Attitudes to Self and School' (PASS) measure from GL Assessment (www.gl-assessment.co.uk/assessments/pass/) is a good starting point, and organisations such as the Anna Freud Centre (mental health; www.annafreud.org/) and Children North East (economic wellbeing; https://children-ne.org.uk/) can be most helpful. The liaison group studies highlight the vital role of pastoral care in helping disadvantaged pupils to thrive academically and socially.

> # ASIDE
>
> ## CASE STUDY: ADDRESSING DISADVANTAGE AT SIR HENRY FLOYD GRAMMAR SCHOOL, BUCKINGHAMSHIRE
>
> ### Context
>
> Sir Henry Floyd Grammar School is a mixed, co-educational grammar school in Aylesbury, Buckinghamshire. The school had put in significant effort to reduce barriers to learning by ensuring that there was no cost of education using PP funding. Poverty-proofing students was at the heart of our previous PP strategy, alongside ensuring that places were made available for disadvantaged students who didn't pass entrance exams. However, there remained a significant academic gap between the outcomes for non-PP students and PP data. I joined SHFGS in 2022 and have worked with Marc on reviewing our strategy through the Buckinghamshire Challenge Network.

Mission statement

Our mission statement for PP centres around the delivery of a contemporary grammar-school education that challenges and inspires everyone to achieve exceptional outcomes. We have to aim to level the playing field. We empower all our students to contribute and engage with all aspects of school life. Through our Floydian Scholar attributes we aim to support our most vulnerable students by offering them opportunities to be resourceful, respectful, resilient, reflective and place an emphasis on reciprocity. We understand that education changes lives, and we have high expectations of our entire school community, including our disadvantaged students. We believe they are capable of changing the world and so we aim to deliver a broad curriculum that inspires students to push past any barriers they may face.

We want all our students to feel safe and secure and we have recognised the critical role that safeguarding and outstanding pastoral support offers our school community. We believe consistency is key and ensure we have clear routines and structures to allow all our students to thrive (https://researchschool.org.uk/durrington/news/levelling-the-playing-field).

The school has tried to remove the deficit discourse around disadvantage and its impact on learning and participation in school life. We recognise that society may have underserved our students and feel privileged in the role we play in ensuring our disadvantaged pupils and their families access the highest quality education they deserve. They are our school community, and we hold them in high regard.

Through the CPD pathways, we have secured a school-wide understanding of how disadvantage impacts on pupils' learning and broader experiences in school. Our staff aim to see school life through the lens of disadvantaged pupils and their families. We have a sharp focus that many of our disadvantaged students have additional vulnerabilities and through assessment and not assumption, we seek to review who our contextual disadvantaged students are to close any gaps. We are ambitious that we pioneer a grammar school education that equips the visionaries of tomorrow and measure that success on the outcomes of our most disadvantaged students.

We then completed data analysis to find three key areas to commit to improve. These areas were:

- attendance
- SEMH
- assessment and outcomes.

In order to have the biggest impact, we ensured that these permeated through individual subject and faculty action plans, alongside our whole-school improvement plan, to share joint agency on improving outcomes for our disadvantaged students.

Practical strategies

We utilised a number of practical strategies and these have included:

- **Attendance officer/outreach officer/EBSA (emotionally based school avoidance) worker:** We managed to secure additional uplifts for staff through PP and secured additional funds through our local authority (high needs block funding or HNBF) to recruit an outreach officer and an EBSA worker. These two roles were trained in EBSA framework, trauma-informed practice and SEND to create bespoke plans to reintegrate students into school. Our EBSA worker also did on-site tuition to enable us to support students returning on site. This also gave our attendance officer capacity to do earlier interventions and robust data analysis to target students with poor attendance. We prioritised daily phone calls home for FSM and PP students.
- **Boxall profiles:** We invested in Boxall profiling using PP funding in order to give more quantitative and qualitative tracking of SEMH needs for students.
- **Increased role of tutor:** We dedicated additional training and guidance for tutors to emphasise the importance of student belonging, especially for the disadvantaged. We utilised 'Walk and Talk' (a weekly form-time walk where

peers walk outside and catch up side by side) as an opportunity for tutors to engage with disadvantaged students to ensure they had resources.

- **EBSA evenings:** We focused on parental outreach and engaging with EBSA parents and those parents from disadvantaged backgrounds. This included hosting training evenings with parents and offering dinner/refreshments as an informal relationship-building opportunity. We did these after school to encourage parents who may find the school site triggering in the day or have work commitments.
- **Academic interventions:** Faculty and subject leaders ran weekly KS4 academic interventions for students underachieving, prioritising SEND and disadvantaged students. These were small-group interventions during form time; support staff covered tutor times in order for this to be facilitated.
- **Chromebook roll out:** All students entitled to PP funding are given a Chromebook free of charge upon enrolment.
- **CPD:** Marc and the team from the local authority ran numerous sessions on supporting PP students and disadvantaged students, and all staff, from the SLT to support staff, engaged in these workshops. We also invested in CPD pathways for staff to focus on supporting disadvantaged students, building belonging, DEI (diversity, equity and inclusion) and SEND.
- **Counselling:** We were able to build a relationship with a local college. This enabled us to have up to 10 trainee counsellors a week, for which we prioritised support to those from disadvantaged backgrounds. We used PP funding to pay for professional supervision for the trainee counsellors.
- **Words matter:** We worked closely with staff to be very mindful of our discourse. We avoid using phrases such as 'PP students', as this label can influence unconscious bias. Within senior leadership, we use the term 'disadvantaged' to refer to those pupils that are underserved by society. We are respectful and mindful of the impact of our language and unconscious bias. PP is a funding mechanism, not a personal character description.

- **NGRT/GL Assessments:** In a bid to focus on assessment and not assumption, we invested in NGRT (New Group Reading Tests) and GL assessments

Outcomes

Provisionally, the outcomes for the year 2023/24 look fantastic. We have been able to report increased attendance across the whole school. We aimed for 2% improvement and achieved 4% in 2024/2025.

Our provisional KS4 data indicates that our disadvantaged students outperformed their non-disadvantaged peers. Their positive progress 8 score is over +0.23% higher than non-disadvantaged. In real terms, this is nearly 1 grade better.

More importantly, however, on average 98% of our students, throughout various times in the year, reported feeling safe in school in student surveys on wellbeing. We build an inclusive and welcoming environment for everyone in our school community.

Katie Evans

TRANSITION

Transition points, particularly between schools, can potentially be a catalyst for change in attendance at school and motivation for learning. The table below is designed to be a starting point for thinking about difficulties with transition, particularly from the perspective of disadvantaged pupils.

Lower attainers	Both	Higher attainers
Reading	Knowledge of families	'What to do when I don't know the answer'
Background knowledge	Consistency of relationships	Comparisons to peers (holidays, etc.)
Vocabulary	Not fitting into any category	Self-esteem
Self-efficacy	Lowering of expectations, associated with labels: 'PP and SEND'	
Social capital	Issues with motivations/ priorities (associated with child development)	
Perception of potential (staff)	Impact of the variable	
Behaviour	Routines and consistency	
Changes to routines		
Changes to relationships		
Issues with independence		
Child development – being 'successful'		

At points of transition, note that:

- transition is a process, not an event
- improving pupils as learners is the most effective strategy
- it is important to keep things manageable (from the perspective of staff, pupils and families)
- it is important to keep things realistic (from the perspective of staff, pupils and families)
- prior attainment should not be an anchor on future attainment
- you should define what success looks like during transition
- staff should know their role in achieving that success (primary and secondary, teaching staff and support staff).

In an article on reading skills for the Royal Holloway University, Professor Jessie Ricketts, from the Department of Psychology, argues that improving pupils' reading attainment is key to effective transition in the long term (2023):

> The connection between reading proficiency and learning new words might seem obvious, but this is the first time this has been demonstrated in a real-life context.
>
> We show that, if we can help children to read more proficiently, then other benefits are likely to follow, such as better learning of new vocabulary and more time spent reading. Similarly, if reading proficiency is low, then children are going to be struggling to learn new words, which will disadvantage them in the transition to secondary school.

SHARING AN UNDERSTANDING OF PUPILS' NEEDS AND INTERESTS

Schools may want to consider information such as that listed below and determine how this information will be communicated to key members of staff:

- the increasing SEND needs across school (not just EHCP information)
- where staff can access CPD, networks about priorities
- details about which pupils are/are not participating in extracurricular activities

- opinions/views that pupils have about extracurricular activities/ enrichment opportunities
- information about why pupils may be reluctant to participate.

For more on transition, particularly about the transition from KS2 to KS3, this video from the Unity Research School may help: https://vimeo.com/962236576/0a6f47738f.

ASIDE

LITERACY AND WHY IT IS FUNDAMENTAL TO SUPPORTING DISADVANTAGED STUDENTS

Understanding the correlation between socioeconomic disadvantage and educational outcomes is important for all us educators, regardless of role or context. But, specifically understanding the relationship between literacy and disadvantage is even more crucial because, without this knowledge, we will never be able to successfully address some of our biggest challenges such as improving attendance, quality of teaching and curriculum, or creating inclusive, equitable and meaningful school experiences for all children and young people. Without this knowledge, we cannot break cycles of disadvantage.

So, what is the link with literacy? Well, pupils often face challenges that make them more vulnerable as learners (readers and writers) and are therefore more likely to need support with their literacy and language. Factors such as limited access to resources, fewer cultural experiences, limited background knowledge, gaps in education and special educational needs can all negatively impact upon pupils' development of language, reading and writing.

Regardless of their background, pupils can also be disadvantaged because of the differential school practices that they encounter, such as quality of teaching, curriculum delivery and attainment grouping. Either way, these are factors beyond the control of the pupil.

Differential practices *are*, however, within the control of schools. If the explicit development of literacy and language is not at the heart of decision-making and at the core of teaching practice, struggling readers and writers will continue to be further disadvantaged because they cannot access or make meaning of the curriculum and other aspects of school life.

There are some very simple and sensible things we can all do in schools to address this, but they require all school leaders to boldly create a culture, climate and capacity conducive to effective literacy provision. The sooner we start talking about how literacy *is* learning, how opportunities for reading and writing need to be *embedded* within learning sequences, and how literacy is the golden thread of our curriculum, the sooner standards of oracy, reading and writing will improve.

Regardless of the phase or subject taught, all educators should provide language-rich environments and opportunities to extend pupils' vocabularies, and plan for high-quality interactions that develop and extend pupils' thinking.

High-quality texts should drive the development of knowledge, and pupils' reading fluency and comprehension should be supported with research-informed approaches. Opportunities and processes to develop writing should be explicit and should support pupils' self-regulation. The key to success is being conscious of the reciprocal relationship between oral language, vocabulary, reading and writing, and to make explicit connections between the domains as they are taught.

These approaches should be integral to every school's development plan, every year. They are not 'nice-to-haves'. Instead, they are critical levers that help to level the playing field, and they should always be top priority. Sadly, if they are not, we are part of the problem.

Sarah Green

UNITING

There tends to be very little difference between schools where disadvantaged pupils are thriving and those where pupils are struggling in terms of the activities taking place in school and in how the PP is spent. The key message here is that it is how well we do things that matters – the practitioner is the intervention. Doing fewer things not only heightens our chances of doing things well, it also creates a strong sense of purpose and avoids overwhelming staff.

Focusing on fewer things is often a good sign of a tight understanding of the needs of pupils. The more things we try to do, the less effective we become.

Where schools struggle to address disadvantage, there is often a focus on operational compliance. Responsibility for disadvantage tends to sit with a small number of people (and that responsibility is often passed around the leadership team frequently). Where disadvantaged pupils thrive, there is a collective understanding of the issues faced by pupils, a collective understanding of how the school is responding, and everyone understands their responsibility in enacting the school's united approach.

Question for reflection:

The PP grant is often tied up in staffing. How are those staff being developed, deployed and supported to improve the learning, personal development and wellbeing of disadvantaged pupils in our settings?

Our work focused on disadvantage demonstrates:

- Pupils with strong language, good background knowledge, self-efficacy and good self-regulation skills can thrive, even if elements of teaching, such as explanations, modelling or relationships, are not always perfect.
- Pupils with more limited language, background knowledge and self-regulation skills need the highest-quality explanations, formative assessment and strong relationships. High-quality, inclusive teaching matters for all pupils, but particularly for those that find learning more difficult.

ASIDE

CASE STUDY: ADDRESSING DISADVANTAGE AT SIGMA TRUST, ESSEX

Improving the quality of education for all pupils is the central strand of Sigma Trust's Improvement Strategy. This is underpinned by our belief that achievement is for all and that no child should be left behind. Our disadvantage strategy to close the achievement gap is led by the Director of School Improvement and is focused on all students who are vulnerable to underachievement, particularly those who are disadvantaged and have special educational needs. It is made up of five elements:

1. Create a trust-wide culture where the challenge of raising achievement for disadvantaged students and those with SEND is acknowledged and embraced.
2. Securing successful learning outcomes is the primary objective. Most focus should be on improving the quality of learning experiences for all students.
3. All students should be supported to make the most of all the opportunities available at school.
4. There is no complacency. School leaders regularly scrutinise the intent, implementation and impact of their strategy.

5. Assumptions are challenged and there is a palpable sense of urgency. Strategy is evidenced-informed with an emphasis on early and effective intervention.

After ensuring that all schools had identified leaders within their schools to drive a multi-disciplinary approach (typically a deputy headteacher), the trust implemented a programme of quality assurance and professional development opportunities to improve colleagues' understanding of all the potential barriers to underachievement. All schools' PP statements are routinely and robustly interrogated to ensure the challenges are accurately identified and the intended outcomes of the plans are ambitious.

Professional development for teachers and support staff has been focused on maximising meaningful student participation (for example, via improved questioning, modelling, scaffolding and language development). This work has taken place from a whole-school perspective and a subject-specialist perspective and is rooted in research as detailed in 'The EEF guide to the Pupil Premium' (2024b). Teacher development is now driven by evidence-informed programmes such as The Great Teaching Toolkit (https://evidencebased.education/great-teaching-toolkit-cpd/) and in partnership with the Ambition Institute (www.ambition.org.uk/). This is being embedded alongside the systematic implementation of Essex Local Authority's 'Ordinarily Available' framework which details high-quality education for SEND and disadvantaged learners.

Building on our approach to develop the professional learning community of SENCOs and provide coordinated specialist training for support staff, all schools in the Sigma Trust are participating in the Whole Education SEND school improvement programme (https://wholeeducation.org/send) to further develop the strategic leadership of SEND and improve outcomes for vulnerable learners. 'Knowing the individual' is at the heart of our schools' approach and to this end, we have invested in trust-wide screening of speech and language needs in Years 3 and 7 as well as reading and writing ability in Year 7 and formal progress tests in Year 9.

This has enabled us to create a programme of intervention based on precise identification of need as well as closer tracking of the 'gap'. This laser focus also extends to pastoral leaders implementing the trust's 'Attendance is Achievement Strategy' to ensure the attendance gap is tackled with precision and urgency. All of this work supports our drive to provide an effective and inclusive education.

Kay Turner

VIOLA

I have chosen the word 'viola' here as this particular instrument is an important part of any orchestra. As educators, we can only orchestrate an effective disadvantage strategy through a deep understanding of how low family income impacts on the learning, wellbeing and personal development of the individual.

The model below breaks down the impact of low family income into three parts.

1. **More visible aspects of disadvantage** – these are readily seen, but are perhaps harder to influence in some cases. They include: poor-quality housing, mobility, access to resources beyond school, poor physical and mental health, lack of structure, an increased likelihood of being a victim of crime or experiencing adverse childhood experiences beyond the school gate.

2. **Less visible, or internal, aspects of disadvantage** – these can be around confidence, social isolation, motivation, fatigue (particularly for lower attainers) or attendance to learning.

3. **Academic aspects** –   relating to language development, background knowledge, self-regulation and more.

The great leveller is the quality of education that pupils experience. The better the quality of education, and the more effectively we implement our disadvantage strategies, the better we can mitigate the impact of low family income beyond the school gate.

THE A–Z OF ADDRESSING DISADVANTAGE

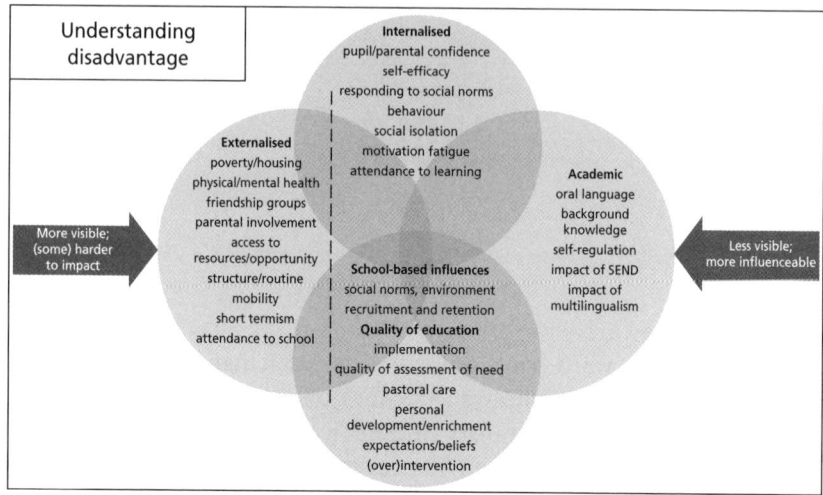

A blank template version of the above figure has been included below for mapping.

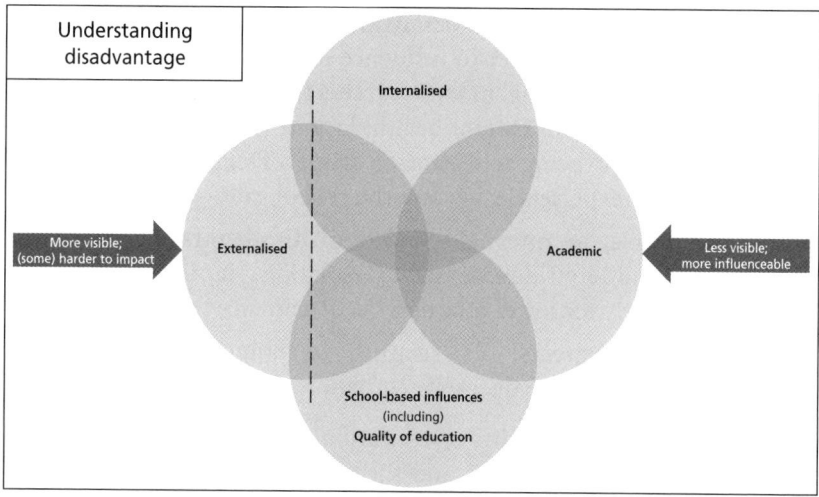

You cannot intervene into a label. You cannot intervene to a symptom. Our work around addressing disadvantage should be about empowering teachers and wider school staff. This will enable pupils to be successful. We need to focus on the highest-leverage approaches (as illustrated in the light grey bubbles in the following figure). We cannot solve all the challenges pupils may face, but we can help them to be better learners. It is absolutely crucial that our teachers feel empowered. If teachers are empowered, pupils will be empowered.

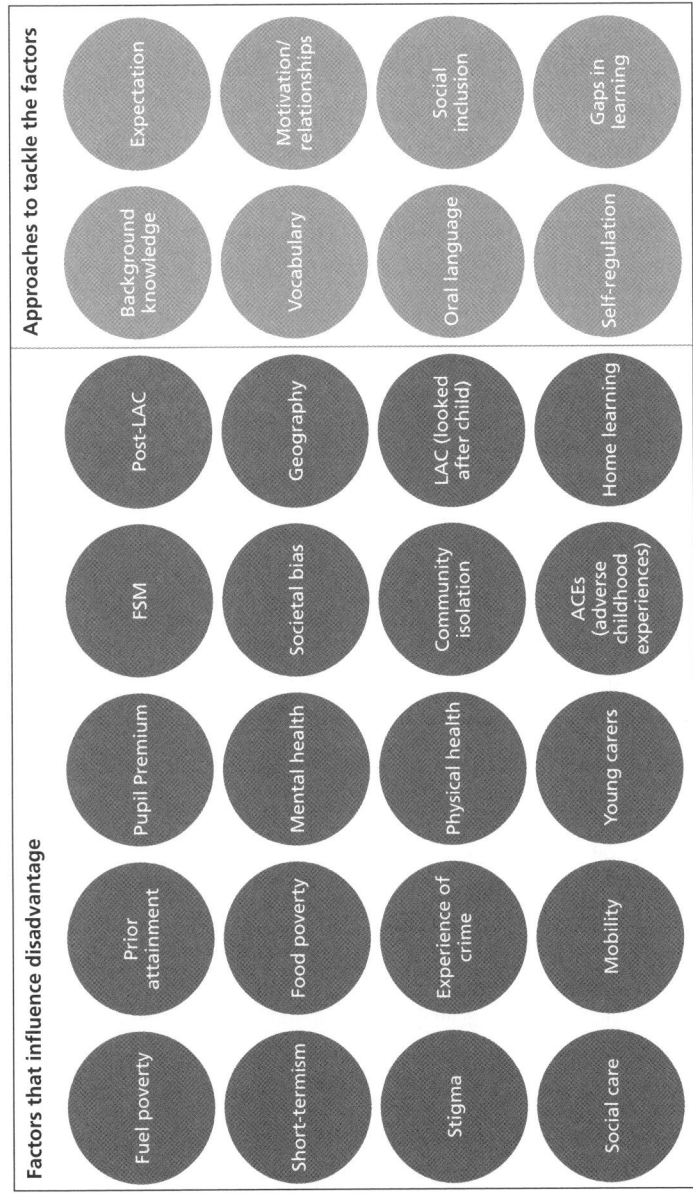

> ## ASIDE
> ### CASE STUDY: ADDRESSING DISADVANTAGE AT TRENANCE LEARNING ACADEMY, CORNWALL
>
> Trenance's approach to addressing disadvantage is ultimately 'what we do for one, we do for all'. Ensuring that we have an engaging, challenging and well-rounded curriculum means that any child that sets foot inside our school has access to the best start in life and provides an opportunity for all pupils to achieve through education. This starts with a rigorous and whole-team focus on attendance. Our mantra is 'every child, in school, on time, learning ready'. Good attendance begins with school being a place where pupils want to be, where they feel safe, feel calm and feel supported by trusted adults.
>
> We are unapologetic with our approach to structure and high expectations. We accept nothing less than the best and make each lesson count. There is no second chance; no 'we'll try that again'. Children have 570 days with us, a set number of lessons that will impact their journey through life, and all of us accept that we need to get this right and provide high-quality teaching each day. This is supported through whole-staff deliberate practice and individual coaching to help teachers to stay up to date with research and always improving! This doesn't mean we lack warmth or 'fun'; we have a very strong personal development programme that enriches our curriculum, develops pupils of all backgrounds and deeply routes each child in their community.
>
> We work closely with our families to build strong, supportive, meaningful relationships so that they see us as those that help, rather than the historic barrier that schools have been known to be. This support extends beyond just getting children to school; we are a hub of support. We help parents with food vouchers, prepare meals, provide washing facilities and offer support with childcare. It is sometimes just as simple as being someone who will listen to them over a cup of coffee.

It's no good having one school giving children the best start, if the one down the road is not offering the same. We work to develop our local community, we work with childcare providers, sports and arts clubs, and businesses to provide events, make connections and ensure that those deemed to be disadvantaged have access to a wider offer outside of the school walls.

As an accredited DfE English Hub and a Voice 21 Centre of Excellence, we firmly believe that reading and oracy are the equaliser to bridging the gap. We focus relentlessly on giving all pupils the ability to read and speak well as this is the gateway to a successful future. Reading sings throughout our school; books are everything and everywhere. We all know the difference that the word gap has on children's development and success later in life, but we can remove this inequality.

Staff and children read daily, we discuss vocabulary (including the meaning and history of words) we link books and texts to all that we do and ensure that all pupils leave Trenance not only able to read but choosing to read for pleasure. Oracy is woven through everything that we do. We ensure that all pupils have the opportunity and skills to develop their speaking and listening. We believe and understand the importance of oracy, that it is more than a skill for life but a gift; a gift that ensures that no matter your background or your lived experience, you can take on future challenges with confidence, with conviction and the belief that your thoughts matter and your opinion counts.

Obviously, none of this can be delivered by one or a few. It takes the whole team – teachers, support staff, administrators, kitchen teams and site teams – to buy in wholeheartedly to the belief that we can, we do and we will continue to give all pupils, but especially those that are deemed to be disadvantaged, the education and support that every child is entitled to.

We collectively understand that we have a civic duty to break the cycle of poverty. We work tirelessly to ensure that everything we offer means that we positively advantage children growing up in disadvantaged environments.

Matt Williams

WORDS

Early intervention and improving pupils as learners are key themes when looking to address educational disadvantage. Our efforts to address disadvantage are hugely influenced by how well children learn to read, and make the transition to reading to learn. Experts Rowena Lucas and Timi Alabi explain why early reading is the key to a successful education, particularly for those pupils growing up in low-income households.

Early reading is a cornerstone for future learning. Children that read well from an early age have a significant advantage in learning at all ages, and all aspects of school life.

If disadvantaged pupils can read well at an early stage, it opens up a world of knowledge and opportunity. Disadvantaged pupils who read well can access information that can improve them as learners, broadening horizons and increasing their background knowledge, and this leads to better achievement.

It gives children exposure to stories and knowledge that they may not normally be able to access because of the circumstances they are growing up in. Reading bridges that opportunity gap.

Early reading is crucial for vocabulary acquisition and language development. It introduces children to a wide range of vocabulary, enhancing their language and cognitive development. As teachers and leaders, we need to focus on the things that we can control; the things that we can impact. We control the school environment and the learning environment, but we can't control many of the things that happen beyond the school gates.

Early reading helps build self-esteem. Pupils who read well early on stand tall. It gives them dreams and goals that they can realise. They don't feel limited. Early readers are confident readers. It's the best start for developing a love of reading too.

Considering reading in its purest form, we need to think about the alphabet code acquisition, and learning to blend to read. But we need to balance that out with a child's own identity as a reader.

The research on self-advocacy and belonging overlaps directly with children's ability to feel that the learning environment is for them. So how are we enabling all pupils – from nursery through to KS4 – to feel like the learning environment they're in is for them? Christopher Such talks about depressurising the classroom environment. So, we need to make sure that children move from learning to read to reading to learn as soon as they can. But, at the same time, we need to ensure that this happens for all children. Children need to have equitable access to the curriculum and wider school life.

So, it is our moral duty to ensure that all children feel a sense of belonging and are equipped to be successful in school. This is true whether it's deciphering squiggles on a page, whether it's how our youngest children learn to use a book, or whether it's a rich discussion about a book. It is important to remember that being part of a community of readers forges a cohesive learning environment. We are inherently social creatures; we like talking to each other and listening to stories. We want all children to have the opportunity to be part of a community. So, as leaders, it is our duty to ensure that they have the environments that are enabling.

We also need to ensure that staff are set up to be successful. We need well-trained, expert staff that know how to accelerate the process of becoming a strong reader as early as possible. This is something that is in our gift as primary educators. We have a wonderful opportunity to change and improve children's lives. How many people get to do that?

Rowena Lucas
Timi Alabi

Promoting good reading habits and building a culture of reading are fundamental to improving pupils as learners, building background knowledge, building cultural and social capital, improving vocabulary and building confidence. Reading is the game changer.

But, promoting a love of reading is not enough. Teaching pupils to read well is fundamental to unlocking enjoyment in reading. Initiatives such as World Book Day and 'Get Caught Reading' are only as effective as the practice of teaching children to learn to read. We rarely enjoy things that we find really difficult, especially when we are struggling compared to our peers. While reading outside of school can support school efforts, if we rely on what pupils do outside of school, we are likely to widen gaps.

Research from the Centre for Longitudinal Studies at University College London (UCL, 2017) has uncovered why reading can help unlock disadvantage. The better we read, the more we want to read and the more success we experience across the curriculum. It is *the* intervention that disadvantaged pupils need.

By analysing the scores of 11,000 14-year-old pupils, researchers concluded that teenagers who read for pleasure in their spare time know 26% more words than those who never read. As a result, teenagers who read often, and those who had access to plenty of books, were more likely to develop a better vocabulary than their peers.

Even taking into account other factors – like the parents' qualifications and profession, and cognitive tests taken by the teenagers when they were aged 5 – teenagers who read for pleasure still got 12% more words right, while those from book-rich homes scored 9%.

'I HAVE FORGOTTEN HOW TO READ'

In an excellent article published in the Canadian newspaper *The Globe and Mail* (2018), an academic called Michael Harris talks about how he's forgotten how to read. This is despite growing up in a book-loving home and being a strong reader into adulthood.

The advent of the smart phone, with its instant gratification and algorithms, means that he is repeatedly shown articles that agree with his opinions. They pull him away from the challenge and joy of reading opinions that challenge his thinking; the texts that broaden his knowledge, rather than narrowing his knowledge. This is a modern phenomenon, and one that we have to grapple with in schools. It is another reason why the fleeting time we have with pupils is so precious.

HOMOPHONES

Background knowledge is language. It is key to success academically and socially. A teacher recently spoke to me about the word 'share', and how it may take on different meanings in different subjects in different aspects of school life. It means something different in play in the early years. It means something different in economics and mathematics. It certainly means something different in PSHE. In some cases, it's a neutral word. In some cases, it's a positive word. In other cases, it's something that we would warn children against. Language is incredibly complex and interesting. It is critical that educators avoid the presumption of language.

Again, remembering that it's **conversation, not word exposure** that builds literacy and language, we need to dump pre-printed vocabulary lists from the internet and build language together with pupils, enabling multiple meaningful interactions with word meanings. This notion was brilliantly articulated in *Bringing Words to Life* (2013).

ASIDE

CASE STUDY: ADDRESSING DISADVANTAGE AT BURNT MILL ACADEMY TRUST, ESSEX/HERTS/EAST LONDON

The approach to supporting our many disadvantaged learners at Burnt Mill Academy Trust (BMAT) is relatively straightforward: we want to improve the quality of teaching. We understand that pastoral and enrichment activities are important, but our main focus needs to be on the area over which teachers and leaders have the most influence: what is happening regularly in our classrooms.

We also understand that language holds the key to unlocking the educational potential of our disadvantaged learners. Reading, oral-language skills and vocabulary development across the curriculum are at the forefront of our approach. Staff are trained and supported, firstly to understand the causes of educational disadvantage and, secondly, the vital role language plays in closing the attainment gap.

BMAT is guided by a clear vision: 'To work together to smash through the barriers that prevent our children from becoming confident, high-achieving and independent individuals.' Central to this vision is a commitment to avoid the labelling of pupils. We try to ensure that all children are seen for their potential rather than their circumstances. The trust supports this approach with its long-term PP strategy. We equip staff with practical strategies to support language development; key initiatives include a consistent approach to the explicit teaching of vocabulary and the implementation of a trust-wide reading strategy.

Well-defined principles of oracy and collaborative learning are also prioritised. Partnerships with Research Schools further enhance evidence-based teaching practices, while trustees focus on accountability of leaders by regularly reviewing the outcomes for learners from marginalised groups.

In partnership with Greenshaw Research School, we developed our secondary reading strategy. The aims of this strategy are to improve our teachers' knowledge of how students learn to read, to increase the amount of time spent reading across the school day (across all subjects) and to improve the quality and delivery of reading materials. The strategy has four components:

1. formalising content by creating reading packs and using quality texts and books, rather than reading from a classroom screen
2. improving vocabulary via explicit vocabulary instruction
3. better utilisation of form tutor reading time which now uses an inclusive reading approach
4. creating a safety net for readers with low attainment by providing a research-based targeted intervention.

For oral language development, the primary schools lead the way. There are robust screening processes in place during the early years phase to identify speech and language needs, and intervene accordingly. A consistent approach to speaking and listening has been developed via our collaborative learning principles which give four key strategies to promoting speaking and listening in class. The schools have been tasked with creating a culture of oracy in their settings, one in which there is an expectation that all pupils will speak regularly and where staff encourage and model speech in all its forms.

BMAT supports those at risk of low attainment due to educational disadvantage. It's not perfect, but as a trust we acknowledge that we are on a journey. Undoing generations of educational disadvantage can feel like thankless work but we take stock regularly and celebrate our successes. Most of all, we remain focused. Whether you are a teacher of science, art or English, consistently good teaching and language development are the keys to ending the cycle of educational disadvantage.

Neil Stirrat

X-FACTOR

ADDRESSING DISADVANTAGE: POINTS FOR DISCUSSION, BASED ON LEARNING FROM SUCCESSFUL SCHOOLS

What can we learn from those schools that seem to have the 'X-factor'; those schools where strategies are making a difference to the lives of disadvantaged learners?

Disadvantage strategies are doomed to difficulty if we neglect:

- excellent teaching and learning within a high-quality, well-sequenced curriculum
- enrichment: building social inclusion and broadening vistas
- a personal development curriculum: building confidence and agency
- wellbeing: supporting good physical and mental health.

Other points to note:

- There is a reality around funding. PP funding is often tied up in staffing, so making sure staff have the knowledge, skills, expertise and support is key.
- We need a national debate about the remit of schools, and wider state provision.
- Nothing is possible if culture, belief and expectation are not right. Teaching disadvantaged pupils should be seen as a privilege, not a problem.
- We are often the variable. We need to be the consistent.
- The purpose of childhood is to be a child!
- The practitioner is the intervention.

- Adopt the mantra of assessment, not assumption.
- Understand low family income. Never limit pupil opportunities based on family income, capacity or behaviours.
- Don't overcomplicate, don't overwhelm. Focus on highest-leverage areas, such as reading. Don't make presumptions in the classroom.
- Give teachers the expertise, knowledge and support to help pupils to thrive.
- If teachers thrive, pupils will thrive. Happy teachers, happy pupils.
- Classrooms are critical, but they are not enough on their own.
- Be sceptical about intervention (while maintaining optimism about what can be achieved).
- Focus on effective implementation.
- Evaluate dispassionately. Understand rather than prove.
- Avoid 'first come, first served' (especially with enrichment).
- Critically engage with research evidence (such as research on class sizes).
- Doing things badly can be worse than not doing things at all (avoid busy-ness!).
- Curriculum content coverage is a poor proxy for learning.
- Getting 30 individual children to learn something is rather complex!
- You see things differently at the back of the class. We need to walk alongside practitioners.
- A 'chaotic home life' is not a diagnostic assessment.
- Reading is the great social justice lever that's in our gift. (Are pupils just reading in reading lessons?)
- Feedback can be a gap widener.
- It's easy to forget to tell experienced staff that they are doing a good job.
- It is absolutely possible for disadvantaged pupils to attain well and thrive in wider school life.
- Being a contributor (to school and community) is the game changer.

Things to remember in all of this. We're brief visitors to the lives of our (disadvantaged) pupils. But we make a huge difference through great teaching and learning, high expectations, belief in their potential, social inclusion, respect, opportunity and kindness (including difficult messages!).

> ## ASIDE
> ### CASE STUDY: ADDRESSING DISADVANTAGE IN A RURAL SCHOOL WITH LOW PUPIL NUMBERS, BROUGHTON PRIMARY SCHOOL, CUMBRIA
>
> In guidance for addressing educational disadvantage, there are often few examples of schools in rural communities with relatively low numbers. The strategy from Broughton Primary in Cumbria is a model of excellence about how to plan to address the disadvantage challenge for a school in this context. The school website gives full details about the strategy used (https://broughtonprimarysch.co.uk/our-school/pupil-premium).
>
> The intent statement sets out what the school is looking to achieve for disadvantaged pupils, and how it will go about achieving it. The language communicates with all stakeholders.
>
> The five challenges in the plan focus on academic, social and pastoral issues. Leaders have 'got below the surface' and have a strong understanding of the links between low income and school life. Addressing these issues will help pupils to thrive in all aspects of school life.
>
> The intended outcomes link directly to the challenges and use both qualitative and quantitative measures (qualitive indicators, rather than percentages, are important with low numbers).
>
> The activity in the plan is detailed, precise and well evidenced. It links with the challenges, and rightly focuses on ensuring the staff have the capacity, expertise and skills to help pupils to thrive.
>
> The clarity/detail in the plan enables leaders to quality assure the effectiveness of provision. Leaders have engaged thoughtfully with evidence to inform decision making.

YAHOO

It is important to celebrate successes and remember that schools are, for the most part, joyful places!

Addressing educational disadvantage is a significant challenge, driven by some factors which are way beyond the control of school. But the underachievement of pupils from low-income households is not inevitable.

Throughout the book, there are examples of colleagues who are overcoming the challenge, enabling disadvantaged pupils to thrive socially and academically. Schools matter. But what really matters is the people within them. Teachers and support staff matter to all children. But they particularly matter to pupils that experience disadvantage.

Despite the challenges, we have a strong knowledge base about how low income impacts academically and socially. We have practitioners, leaders, schools and groups of schools who make it their mission to help disadvantaged pupils to thrive. Not so they can escape their communities, but so they can be positive contributors to their communities.

Teachers, wider staff teams, leaders and schools have faced a pretty bumpy road in the last 10 years: political instability, social unrest, global pandemics, the rise of the smartphone, vapes, cost of living crises, global conflict, climate change, the age of misinformation, stressed families, toxic masculinity, the medicalisation of normal life, cuts to social care provision and more. Yet classrooms and schools remain great places to be. Schools should be places that are full of fun and joy and laughs and kindness.

As one interaction with a pupil in Reception class went recently:

Pupil: 'Hello ... what's wrong with your nose?'
Me: 'Nothing, I don't think ...'
Pupil: 'It's REALLY big!'
Teacher: 'Everything is big when you are four.'

As Phil Stock, Director of Greenshaw Research School (and a great champion for addressing disadvantage), says:

> While every school has its own contextual factors to attend to, and is at a different stage of its development, all schools can benefit from a collaborative approach to development, particularly in terms of sustaining long-term changes to culture or practice. It's people (the teachers, the support staff and the pupils) that ultimately make the biggest difference.

ASIDE

CASE STUDY: ADDRESSING DISADVANTAGE AT SAMARES SCHOOL, JERSEY

Our approach is to ensure that our school development strategy and Jersey [pupil] premium strategy are one and the same.

We have five clear priorities. They benefit all pupils, but particularly those experiencing disadvantage:

1. High-quality teaching
2. Curriculum development
3. Developing and sustaining a language-rich environment
4. Supporting mental health and wellbeing
5. Improving behaviour and personal development.

Within each of these priorities, there are specific structures, actions, projects, aims and objectives to achieve. All staff know what our focus is on. This means that our approach to disadvantage is consistent, unconditional and universal. Our approach is not a list of extras that staff have to do. It's about empowering staff – a collective responsibility for enacting the school vision.

Oracy education has been transformative. Every voice is heard and valued. All staff are behind the approach. All staff are committed to developing themselves and their pupils. Seeing the impact of this work has driven motivation.

Oracy has helped academic learning and personal development; pupils can articulate how they feel through words and discussion. It has supported them to be successful in school, but it has extended beyond the school and into the wider community.

Developing a high-quality curriculum is fundamental. We have good attendance, but want to make sure that every moment counts. Every moment is a learning moment – in the classroom and during unstructured times.

We are intentional about everything. We have a behaviour curriculum – in the classroom and beyond. Every moment is a teachable moment. Memorable interactions for pupils every day.

We also think about the importance of the school within the community. We have worked to build strong relationships with our community. We have opened up the school to the community, and are front facing around food, shelter and building a culture of trust. We are an unwavering, dedicated team committed to serving our families to help them to thrive.

George Lumley

ZEITGEIST

ATTENDANCE (THE BIG THING EVERYONE IS WRESTLING WITH!)

Disadvantaged pupils and those with special educational needs are more likely to be absent from school.

Published in September 2024, Transforming Attendance in Cornwall focuses on how schools have been addressing the attendance challenge in rural, coastal and town communities. It is rooted in research evidence and the lived experiences of schools, pupils and families. Details are provided in the references section at the end of this book.

In the report, there are nine recommendations, with detailed, practical, evidence-informed guidance and many case studies – from pupil level to trust level – focusing on things that are in a school's gift. Addressing the attendance challenge creates a cohesive school community, and getting it right reduces workload and improves relationships between pupils, families, teachers and leaders.

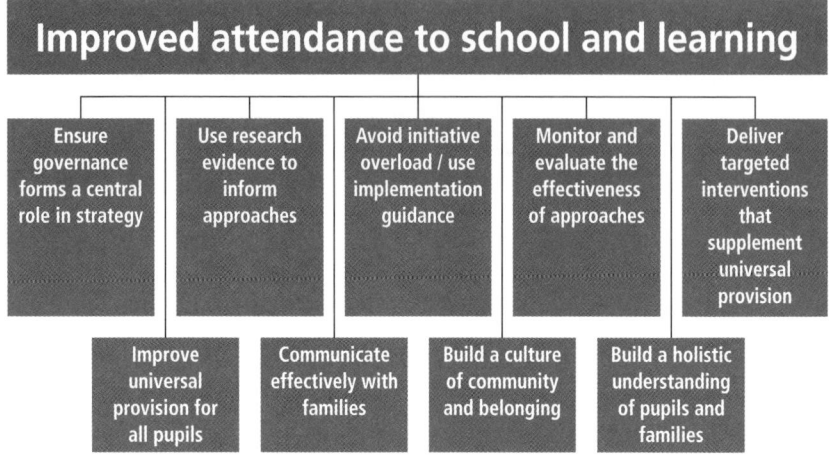

Strategies to address the issues of non-attendance to school and learning

The recommendations, as illustrated in the figure, are as follows:

1. **Use research evidence to inform approaches**. The evidence from securing behaviour change is mixed, context specific, changes depending on the age of pupils, is sometimes counterintuitive and challenges common practices.
2. **Avoid initiative overload**. Keeping it simple is key. The EEF's implementation guidance (2024a) provides a very clear framework for success.
3. **Ensure governors play a central role**. The National Governance Association's guidance is included.
4. **Communicate effectively with families**. Avoid jargon, use neutral, non-judgemental language and build a partnership with families.
5. **Build a holistic understanding of pupils and families**. Assessment, not assumption! Understand the levels that will provoke behaviour change.
6. **Improve universal provision**. In the classroom, in personal development, with enrichment and in wider school life. Schools should be joyful places!

7. **Build a culture of community and belonging**. For *all* pupils, not just those that engage with school life more confidently and readily. Building that culture of community as early as possible is key to success.
8. **Deliver targeted interventions**. Interventions should be evidence-informed, they should motivate and include pupils and families, and they should supplement, rather than supplant, universal provision.
9. **Monitor and evaluate the effectiveness of approaches**. Evaluation is fundamental to continued improvement and better outcomes for pupils and families.

Absence from school life is about more than just coming into the building. There is:

- not coming to school (extended/inconsistent?)
- coming to school but not attending (some) lessons
- poor punctuality to lessons
- exiting the lesson during challenging learning
- coming to lessons but opting out of learning.

And:

- not participating in extracurricular activities, residentials, etc.
- not participating in personal development opportunities – e.g. work experience, student leadership
- not participating in wider school life – e.g. sports teams, music, etc.
- opting out of additional academic support.

Poor attendance at school impacts on pupils academically, socially and in terms of their personal development and their wellbeing. Proactive approaches – linked to pupils experiencing success, feeling like they belong and having strong relationships with adults and peers – are critical.

We need to properly understand the drivers of attendance issues before taking any action. Issues with attendance to school and attendance to learning are symptoms, rather than the issue itself. 'In-school drivers' need to be addressed alongside working with families to ensure sustainable success.

DRIVERS OF NON-ATTENDANCE

In-school drivers can include:

- high turnover of staff – leadership and classroom
- poor staff attendance – academic and pastoral
- several changes in governance approaches – e.g. re-brokering
- inconsistencies in quality of teaching and learning, and pastoral care
- a lack of clarity within school about roles and responsibilities for addressing attendance challenges
- a lack of knowledge and understanding about individual families
- judgemental, inconsistent or inaccessible communications about attendance
- decisions based on labels, rather than need
- lack of (inclusivity).

Community drivers can include:

- geography – transport, population density, local interest (e.g. coastal)
- local housing
- curriculum relevance
- employment levels
- career opportunities
- mobility
- housing
- levels of education in the community
- provision from community services – e.g. health, social care, sport and culture enrichment.

Drivers related to pupils and families can include:

- systemic/attitudinal issues (e.g. term-time holidays)
- low current attainment impacting on confidence, motivation and relationships
- poor reading skills/attainment
- poor behaviour/learning behaviours
- pupils not experiencing success beyond the classroom – e.g. student leadership, sports
- narrow friendship groups
- socially isolated families
- low income and its impact on pupils inside and outside of school
- misconceptions about school attendance in the family
- historic experiences within the family.

These issues impact pupils academically, in their personal and social development.

Understanding the drivers for poor attendance is key to effective mitigation. A video about understanding the drivers can be found here: https://vimeo.com/900841929/6e529b5e30.

THE A–Z OF ADDRESSING DISADVANTAGE

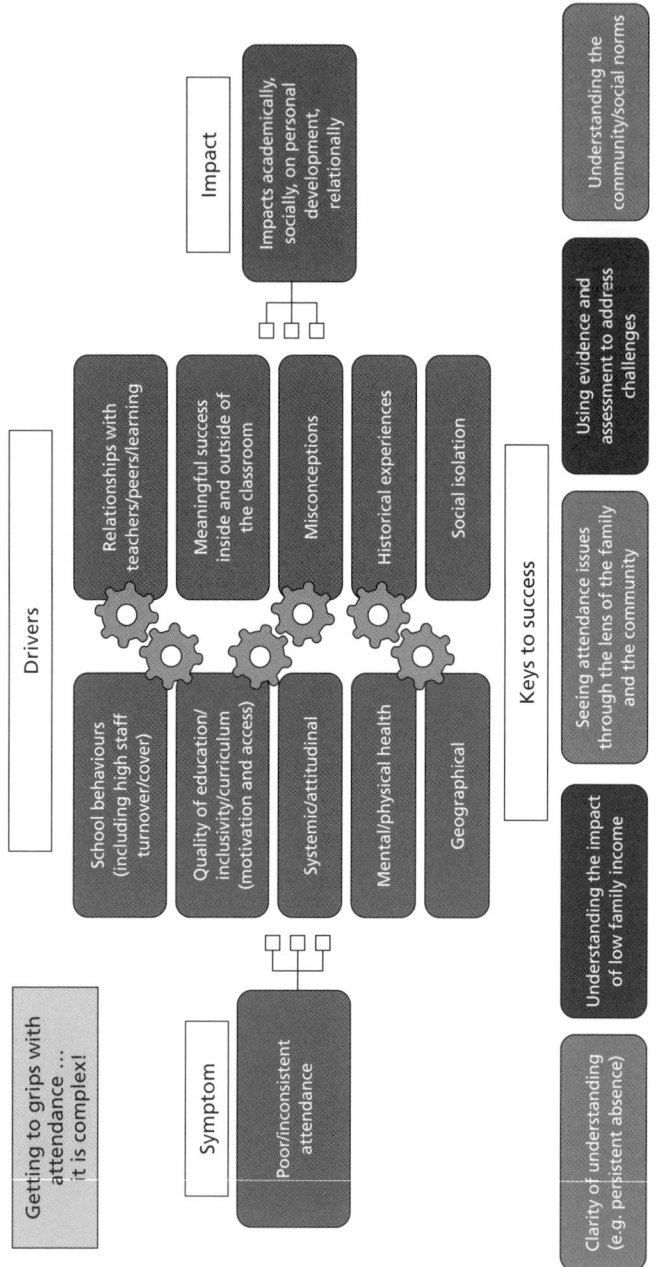

The drivers for poor attendance

The drivers of poor attendance should inform the approaches adopted. The following are examples of how we can be responsive to particular drivers, recognising that some pupils experience multiple drivers. The following examples may be helpful. (The Cornwall report provides more detail.)

DRIVER: PHYSICAL/MENTAL HEALTH

ACTIVITY:

- Class teachers and tutors building relationships: 'I can't wait to see you tomorrow'.
- Carefully modifying language to avoid judgement.
- Offering soft starts/flexibility.
- Ensuring that pupils have strong friendships and are supported in unstructured times.
- Consistent, trusted adults.
- Ensuring pupils are given opportunities in enrichment and student leadership.
- Collective, rather than individual, rewards.
- Rewards for improvement and meeting thresholds, rather than just for achieving the highest grades.

DRIVER: SYSTEMIC/ATTITUDINAL

ACTIVITY:

- Class teachers and tutors building relationships: 'I can't wait to see you tomorrow'.
- Carefully modifying language to avoid judgement: 'We want your child in school – let's work together'.
- Highlighting social norms: pupil attendance compared to that of classmates.
- Highlighting wider challenges arising from poor attendance beyond academic learning: friendships, participation in sport, etc.

- Consistent, trusted adults.
- Attendance induction for families, including problems arising from short-termism: messaging about valuing educational expectance, clarity over consequences, high expectations.
- Use of text messaging rather than letters.
- Reducing jargon.
- Rewards for improvement and meeting thresholds, rather than just for achieving the highest grades.
- Requirement to speak to a person – rather than leave a message – to report absence.
- Pre-emptive support.

EXTRINSIC REWARDS

Extrinsic rewards can have their place as part of a wider attendance strategy. Collective, rather than individual, rewards may be more effective. While rewards for 100% attendance are good for celebrating good attendance, they are unlikely to drive behaviour change for inconsistent attenders, as they do not address underlying drivers. Furthermore, once pupils miss a day, they no longer have an incentive to attend. With 100% attendance awards, we also need to be wary of the 'reward and relax effect', where pupils/families feel they have earned a 'day off' school when attendance has been good over time. Rewards for consistent attendance, as well as improvements in attendance, can be helpful – both in terms of a culture and for good attenders to be 'noticed'.

EVERYONE IS RESPONSIBLE

This 2024 article from Town End Research School exemplifies how all staff can play a role in supporting good attendance through communication with families:

https://researchschool.org.uk/news/think-it-through-thursdays-supporting-pupil-attendance-through-staff-communications

Everyone who works in schools, in any role, has some connection to attendance. Everyone plays a part in supporting school leads to improve attendance, whether or not they are employed in a role directly linked to the management of attendance or attendance-related interventions. Supporting attendance is a whole team effort and it's important to empower all staff members to help in this shared endeavour.

RELATIONSHIPS AND UNDERSTANDING

Clarity over systems and structures is fundamental to success. But this is not enough. We also need to build strong relationships with families and have good two-way communications. We need to properly understand why pupils may be finding it more difficult to attend. Depending on the needs of pupils and families, there are some relatively small changes that can be made that can have a big impact, but some families may need some more intensive support.

In their report 'Behaviour change: School attendance, exclusion and persistent absence' (2017), The British Psychological Society identified four 'factor categories' that can influence attendance. These are physical-health related, mental-health related, systemic or attitudinal issues, and school-behaviour related. Families may experience some or all of these. Low-income families may be more likely to experience physical- or mental-health challenges. Attitudinal issues may be related to lower levels of literacy or difficulties with communication and language. School-behaviour issues may be related to a lack of consistency with attendance approaches, poor relationships with families, poor staff attendance, or judgemental or negative communications. There may also be a lack of understanding of why pupils may not attend.

When discussing issues around attendance with schools nationally, there was a consistent pattern. Pupils whose families feel that they are part of the school community, where those pupils are experiencing success academically and socially, are better motivated to attend. Meaningful participation and meaningful success lead to motivation. 'Upstreaming', providing early support and social inclusion, can help. Every interaction matters: between pupils and pupils, between pupils and adults, and between adults and families. Teachers and pastoral staff must work together too. Teacher and pupil interactions are the glue that makes attendance strategies stick. All families want their children to be successful in school, academically and socially, but sometimes, when experiencing the insecurity of low family income and all that it brings, we are pushed into short-termism.

Stephen Tierney (2017), who has been the driver of some of the most impressive work in addressing disadvantage nationally, writes about the importance of the following:

- Making sure communication about attendance is accessible to families.
- Emphasising the social norm: for example, 'Pupil X's attendance is 87% compared to an average attendance for her peers of 93%. This means that pupil X is missing out on both learning and social time compared to her peers'.
- Partnership: 'Pupil X's attendance *really* matters to us. How can we work together ...?'

Extrinsic rewards need care. They can exasperate issues. Low-stakes, collective rewards for attendance that reaches a threshold, rather than the highest-attending pupil/class, will tend to be more effective. Pupils experiencing success – through personal agency – is important. Rewards for perfect attendance are unlikely to influence behaviour change, neither are raffles (because they are mostly out of pupils' control).

Key reflection: how do we ensure pupils with poor attendance:

- achieve meaningful success, academically, personally and socially
- build strong friendships
- experience joy in the school day?

Do families hear positive messages about their child at school? Every interaction is an attendance intervention. Every conversation is an investment. Cassie Pamplin from Portreath Primary School in Cornwall exemplifies the importance of inclusive communication in this video: www.youtube.com/watch?v=kCd8soHmTkw.

ATTENDANCE AND SAFEGUARDING

School attendance is a safeguarding issue. Regular, frequent attendance at school helps ensure the safety, wellbeing, personal development and academic development of pupils.

When a pupil is absent from school frequently, or for extended periods, it can be an indicator of underlying problems that may put the pupil at risk.

1. **Visibility of pupils:** Schools provide a structured environment where children are regularly seen by teachers and staff who can observe their wellbeing. Any issues between pupils can be picked up within that structured environment.

2. **Early identification of issues:** Teachers and school staff are trained to identify early signs of concern. If a pupil is frequently absent, it can hinder the ability of staff to spot these signs and intervene early.

3. **Monitoring physical, emotional and mental wellbeing:** Schools play a critical role in the physical, mental and emotional development of children. Good attendance allows school staff to recognise changes in behaviour, mood or social interactions that could indicate struggles or concerns.

4. **Access to support services:** Schools provide access to key support services like counselling, social and emotional support, or additional help with academic learning. Poor attendance may mean that a pupil misses out on essential support that addresses need.

5. **Preventing risky behaviour:** Pupils who are frequently absent from school may become vulnerable to risky behaviours or exploitation, especially if their absences are not well supervised. Pupils talking about risky behaviours can be more readily picked up if they are at school.

6. **Enables good communication and understanding:** Good attendance enables teachers and support staff to communicate effectively with pupils, families and other agencies. It enables staff to understand any challenges pupils are experiencing beyond school, and put support or contingency in place. Knowledge of a pupil and their lived experiences enables schools to play their role in keeping children safe.

RESOURCES

Here are some resources that might support efforts to improve attendance in school and attendance to learning:

- DfE attendance resources: www.gov.uk/government/publications/working-together-to-improve-school-attendance
- EEF attendance resources: https://educationendowmentfoundation.org.uk/education-evidence/leadership-and-planning/supporting-attendance
- The Research Schools Network: https://researchschool.org.uk/
- National Governance Association attendance guidance: www.nga.org.uk/knowledge-centre/improving-school-attendance/
- Education Policy Institute reports on attendance: https://epi.org.uk/
- ImpactEd reports and resources: https://lp.impacted.org.uk/
- The Centre for Social Justice attendance report: www.onecornwall.co.uk/attachments/download.asp?file=230&type=pdf
- The Anna Freud Centre (mental health support for children and families): www.annafreud.org
- One Cornwall report: www.onecornwall.co.uk/page/?title=Transforming+Attendance+in+Cornwall&pid=251

ASIDE

CASE STUDY: ADDRESSING DISADVANTAGE AT CITY ACADEMY WHITEHAWK, BRIGHTON

We work in an area where 81% of children live in the top 10% of the most deprived children in the country.

Key is understanding that no single thing will address this challenge. As a team, we must be committed to a whole-school approach to everything we do. And we must do it well.

Historically, things did not work so well at our school. Not because people were not working hard, but because people had applied to work at the school because they thought they wanted to 'save' children.

We needed to move away from that world view because it does not empower pupils. Many of our families feel disempowered. We need to be able to motivate, inspire and challenge children so they are successful. With wellbeing and welfare, but also with academic outcomes.

We built a team that committed to a vision that all children can achieve personal excellence. We recognise that at least two-thirds of children entering school have significantly delayed development. So, for ambitions to be achievable for children, and for staff responsible for those children, we focus on the idea that 'people like me produce excellent work and can do excellent things'.

We have built a team that understands that effectiveness in their role is determined by their role:

> We want you to come here and teach. We will appoint a welfare team to lead on welfare. Your job here is to teach and so by keeping everybody in their lane and having a shared vision that children will achieve excellence, your children achieve excellence.

This meant we had to become system heavy as a school. We were experiencing turbulence in turnover because we were so insistent the children could achieve academically. So, staff were recruited on the premise that they bought into what we are looking to achieve. We are clear about the way we expect children to learn to read. We are clear about how we expect children to develop their writing, in order that they do well. We characterised excellence as a writer. Teachers know what they expect for the children, and they know the little steps needed to get there.

We define everything, to enable staff to experience success. Our well-designed curriculum defines progression in every subject area. This means that we are able to lead children to personal excellence. All children can produce excellent work.

> We build a team by giving them the tools to go on and be successful. By doing this, our children are successful every day. They leave school with strong academic outcomes and are empowered with a keen sense of self-worth.
>
> **Thomas McMorrin**

SECTION TWO

1. RESEARCH SCHOOL NETWORK ARTICLES

The following articles by Marc Rowland were first published through work with the Research School Network. They have been included as 'snapshots' of some of the themes in this book.

1. DfE REPORTING

The DfE PP strategy template aims to provide a much more purposeful approach to accountability. The template is about communicating to internal and external stakeholders, including families, advisers and inspectors. But it should be far more than 'filling out the form'. Rather, individual sections should follow a logic model approach, in line with the Research School programme 'making the difference for disadvantaged pupils'. This article will walk school leaders, and those responsible for PP, through some key reflection points to consider when completing the document, using a worked example.

At the risk of stating the obvious, what we publish on our school website does not address the entrenched issue of educational disadvantage. But the structures and systems we put in place at a strategic level provide the environments for teachers and pupils to thrive together in the classroom. It is in the classroom where we address educational disadvantage. That's where we have the greatest level of influence.

My hope is that the template, and this article, will help school leaders to ask good questions in planning, implementing and evaluating their approach.

The most effective strategies focus on:

- Having the highest of expectations of all pupils, irrespective of background. Remember that disadvantaged pupils don't lack talent or ability, but can lack opportunity. Prior attainment should not set limits on our ambitions for pupils.
- A culture of collective responsibility for disadvantaged pupils, including governance, senior leadership, subject leadership, phase leadership, the classroom (where we really make the difference) and pastoral care.
- A strategy rooted in assessment, not assumptions, of disadvantaged pupils.
- A strategy rooted in addressing the controllable factors that are preventing disadvantaged pupils from attaining as well as they could.
- A learning-led approach, not a label-led approach. Pupils are not at risk of underachievement because they are 'Pupil Premium' or any other label, but because of the impact of socioeconomic disadvantage on their learning over time. This is a long-term process, not an event.
- A culture of early intervention for addressing need, using an evidence-informed, tiered model of teaching and learning, academic intervention and wider approaches. Remember that strategies to address disadvantage stand or fall on how well pupils learn to read. If pupils struggle to read at home, how well we do this in school matters more than ever. Language and social interaction are at the heart of an effective strategy.
- Avoiding 'over-intervention' and recognising the importance of curriculum equity. A narrow curriculum risks double disadvantage and the Matthew effect in action.
- Teacher voice/agency in developing the strategy is vital.
- Effective strategies give teachers and support staff the capacity, knowledge, expertise and support to enable disadvantaged pupils to experience success in challenging learning over time. Addressing disadvantage is not about big, one-off interventions. Every interaction matters and the quality of what we do is critical.

- Avoiding trying to do too many things at once or trying to solve all of society's problems. There should be a strong focus on implementation. The disadvantage strategy should be the wider-school improvement strategy through the lens of disadvantaged pupils and families.
- A clear process and impact evaluation framework, not linked to accountability. Not trying to prove that things are successful, but trying to understand whether it is working/has worked.
- Evaluation frameworks being put in place at the start of the strategy.

2. EVALUATING YOUR PUBLISHED DfE PUPIL PREMIUM STRATEGY

Evaluation should focus on effective processes, as well as outcomes. The process is critical for ensuring that disadvantaged pupils are thriving in the classroom and attaining well.

Process evaluation

Intent

- Has your 'intent' statement created a shared understanding of ambitions, and the principles that underpin your school's strategy for addressing disadvantage?
- Is there a shared understanding of global objectives for disadvantaged pupils – from governance to pastoral care to the classroom? This is something that all school staff should understand.
- Does everyone in school believe that disadvantaged pupils can thrive in the classroom and attain well? Does everyone buy in?

Challenges

- Have you accurately identified the needs of the disadvantaged pupils in your school? The impact of disadvantage on learning is a process, not an event. Neither is it static. Some families may not be significantly economically disadvantaged but may be exceptionally stretched/time poor, or they may be impacted by factors outside of their control. Disadvantage goes beyond the PP label.
- Be wary of negative language about disadvantaged pupils and their families in the challenges section.
- Ensure that challenges are precise.
- Key questions to consider – have we effectively assessed:
    - how disadvantage impacts on pupils' learning (in the individual school context)
    - what the 'controllable' factors impacting on disadvantaged pupils' learning are
    - what factors are *most* preventing disadvantaged pupils from thriving in the classroom and in wider school life?

Intended outcomes and success criteria
- Well-defined success criteria are key to dispassionate impact evaluation.
- Vague success criteria make it easier to claim success. Remember that colleagues involved in the implementation of an approach are not always the best judges of success. Be wary of activity being mistaken for outcomes.
- The intended outcomes should link closely to the challenges pupils face.
- It is important to be mindful of success criteria that are actually activities. For example: 'Learning support reports are produced as soon as possible for children that need them. The information in the reports is shared with parents and used to plan in-class (and small-group) activities and interventions.' While these reports may well be extremely useful and their consistent use may be an indicator that an approach is being implemented effectively, long-term goals should centre on pupils' learning.

Activity
- Activity should link to challenges and intended outcomes/success criteria. The activity section uses the EEF's tiered model. There is no longer any need to list the individual costs of activities, just the budget associated with each tier.
- Schools should link activities with challenges and ensure that activity is informed by research evidence so that it may be effective. Remember that research evidence can only point us in the right direction. We should use it to inform our decision making, not justify it or use it superficially. Research evidence does not just have to come from the EEF toolkit.
- Check that the teaching and learning tier focuses on the challenges identified through assessment.
- When evaluating activity, consider the following (based on the work of Thomas Guskey, 2002):
    - staff acquisition of new knowledge and expertise
    - staff use of new knowledge and expertise

- organisational support/not implanting too many things
- impact on pupils as learners.

• Avoid trying to do too many things at once. This can lead to poor implementation and weaker outcomes. Ensure that activity is focused on helping pupils to be better learners:
  - improving reading comprehension
  - ensuring pupils receive meaningful feedback that they can act on
  - meaningful checking for understanding and responsive teaching
  - exceptionally high-quality pastoral care (including supporting good attendance); many pupils face multiple challenges before they even arrive at school
  - excellent personal development curriculum ensuring that pupils have meaningful interactions with their peers and build strong friendships
  - ensuring that pupils are able to participate in extracurricular opportunities, enrichment, residentials and wider opportunities to build social stories – the joyful, emotional memories of school life that everyone should experience.

• We must be careful about implementation, avoiding trying to do too many things at once, stuck in a cycle of 'outerventions' that impact on pupils academically and socially. As a team, as schools, as a group of schools, we need to Engage, Unite, Reflect, in line with the latest guidance on implementation.

• There should be a dispassionate impact evaluation, focused on the impact on pupils as learners. A robust process and impact evaluation framework should be adopted at the start of support, so teachers and leaders can accurately assess its effectiveness. Changes and adaptations can then be made to the practice and strategy where necessary.

3. 25 STEPS TO SUCCESS
1–7: School culture, expectations …

1. Remove the deficit discourse around disadvantage and its impact on learning and participation in school life. Disadvantaged pupils and their families are not a problem to be resolved. They are our school community and held in high regard. Work in partnership to ensure everyone feels they belong, in all aspects of school life. Be mindful of the risk of a 'school within a school', where school life works for the vast majority of pupils, but a small number are on the margins.

2. Secure a school-wide understanding of how disadvantage impacts on pupils' learning and broader experiences in school. See school life through the lens of disadvantaged pupils and their families. This is important, irrespective of the numbers of disadvantaged pupils in the school.

3. Secure a school-wide understanding of the school's main priorities for addressing disadvantage, and how those priorities present across the curriculum and in wider school life.

4. Focus on issues that are within the school's gift. Focus on issues that are controllable. Limit priorities to those that are most preventing pupils from thriving in the classroom and in wider school life.

5. Coherence and credibility are key to effective implementation in the classroom. Professional development for staff – in academic and pastoral roles – should centre on helping staff to help disadvantaged pupils to thrive in school.

6. Ensure that high-quality, experienced, expert staff are working equitably with disadvantaged pupils, especially those that are lower current attainers. Recruitment, retention and development of staff are fundamental to an effective strategy. This requires a long-term view, with some schools adopting a 'pipeline' approach to teacher recruitment and putting in place high-quality professional-development programmes for all staff, including teaching assistants, teachers of all levels of experience, middle leaders and senior leaders. The same applies to staff in pastoral roles.

7. Ensure, across school, that there is a clear, collective understanding of (and a consistent language lexicon for):
   - high expectations
   - high-quality teaching
   - inclusivity.

8–15: Assessment

8. Use research evidence to inform decision making and challenge plans during planning and implementation. Link exploration of evidence to issues arising from a rigorous assessment of needs. Evidence should inform how schools respond to pupil need in the classroom and in wider school life. A research-informed approach without a rigorous assessment of need may take schools in the wrong direction. Planning and implementation should be firmly embedded in realities of an individual school context.

9. Assessment, not assumption, is at the heart of an effective approach. Assessment of need is not something that is only done before a strategy is implemented. It is a critical ingredient of an effective strategy. Start with the needs of the individual pupils, and build a strategy around emerging themes and common issues. Avoid looking for themes to address with a ready-made solution. Pupil need, not labels, should inform all decision making. Many pupils in our schools that are not eligible for the PP will be experiencing disadvantage. Schools are best placed to determine how disadvantage impacts on pupils in their local communities.

10. Rigorous assessment promotes early intervention and ongoing support for pupils. Early intervention, rooted in pupil need, that enables pupils to thrive in the classroom can prevent curriculum narrowing and a reactive approach.

11. Respond to assessment of need within teaching and learning, as well as interventions. Identifying issues such as pupils' reading age should elicit a response across the curriculum, not just through reading interventions and whole-school reading programmes.

12. Build knowledge of high-quality practice based on effective processes and implementation of evidence-informed strategies. How to do things matters.
13. Ensure that curriculum leaders, subject leaders and pastoral leaders are heavily involved in the planning and implementation of the school's disadvantage strategy as early as possible. Staff in these roles are fundamental to long-term success. Ensure expertise is well utilised.
14. Ensure that the appropriate administrative staff are involved in the planning and implementation stages. Again, these staff are fundamental to long-term success.
15. Streamline approaches by working with external expert partners, both for academic and pastoral approaches. Avoid too many priorities.

16–23: Priorities

16. Build staff expertise around high-priority themes to help pupils to be better learners.
17. Build partnerships and harness local expertise. Supplement teacher expertise. Look for area-based solutions for:
    - curriculum enrichment: museums, theatre, music
    - proactive physical- and mental-health support through expert partners
    - academic support through tuition programmes
    - school development through partnership: local authorities, research schools, hubs, other school-improvement providers; also, within and across multi-academy trusts and with other partners – for teacher expertise, coaching, peer review and dispassionate quality assurance.
18. Improve reading standards. Pupils will read with the breadth, depth and frequency they need to thrive in the classroom if they become strong readers. Our efforts to address disadvantage pivot on how well pupils develop their reading comprehension skills.

19. Poverty proofing is a key ingredient of inclusive schools where disadvantaged pupils are thriving. This should cover both the formal and informal curriculum, as well as uniform, equipment and other resources.
20. Access to the curriculum is not dependent on family resources or income, for example field studies in geography.
21. Pupils should be supported to have good friends and have meaningful interactions with peers across socioeconomic groups.
22. Pupils should have excellent careers education and be involved in meaningful enrichment opportunities. High-quality careers education should not rely on personal networks or social capital. Pupils should play a strong role in wider school and have leadership roles. This can be done through early (and ongoing) involvement in activities that promote self-efficacy and belonging. Being involved in teams (not just sport) and student councils that promote pupil voice on a range of issues can help pupils to feel confident and empowered. Belonging and a sense of place at school should go beyond the classroom.
23. Schools are enhanced and enriched through inclusivity. Inclusion improves schools. It enhances our values and our practices.

24–25: Evaluation

24. Governors should play a key role in rigorous, dispassionate impact evaluation. Decouple impact evaluation from accountability. Evaluation is understanding whether strategies are working, not proving that they are. Evaluation frameworks should be put in place at the start of implementation, not done retrospectively.
25. Adopt evidence-informed approaches to implementation, remembering that the practitioner is the intervention. The EEF guidance resources are the gold standard for this. Again, implementation plans should be rooted firmly in an individual school's context.

4. EEF PRIMARY SCIENCE REPORT

There are six recommendations within the excellent report 'Improving primary science' published by the EEF (2023). They are important for supporting the achievement of all pupils, including those from disadvantaged backgrounds. We focus on four of those here.

They are:

1. Develop pupils' scientific vocabulary

A vocabulary gap for some disadvantaged pupils is something that is familiar to teachers and support staff. It is something teachers will recognise – again, a reflection of the inequalities in social capital and broader experiences, driven by a lack of financial capital. It is certainly not driven by a lack of love or care. The gap is also well documented in the study 'Low income and early cognitive development in the UK' (Waldfogel and Washbrook, 2010).

Vocabulary is something that features in many PP strategies. But how well we teach vocabulary learning in the classroom matters most. The practitioner is what matters most – hence this recommendation 1 must sit alongside recommendation 6.

We need to bring key scientific vocabulary to life with multiple, meaningful interactions, in pupil-friendly contexts (hence the importance of recommendation 4). The etymology can be so powerful: photosynthesis comes from 'photo' = light and 'synthesis' = to compose. Remember, conversation not word exposure builds pupils' language.

Explicitly teach the key vocabulary pupils are going to need to be successful in their lessons. Pre-teach to build confidence if necessary. Intervention that motivates and includes, rather than isolates.

2. Encourage pupils to explain their thinking, whether verbally or in written form

Answers in pupils' books, or on their mini whiteboards, are a poor proxy for learning. Getting pupils to articulate, or write, their thinking:

- Encourages metacognitive learning: How did I achieve that learning? What processes did I go through? Use classroom resources to refer to prior learning.
- Helps teachers to know that pupils are secure in their understanding.
- Stops other pupils from thinking that those that understand the learning are 'magically' clever: 'she's just smart ... she just knows...'.

3. Guide pupils to work scientifically

4. Relate new learning to relevant, real-world contexts

Bringing learning to life in relevant, pupil-friendly contexts supports motivation, confidence building and a sense of purpose. 'This is relevant to me in my community.' 'How might we understand energy sources in Cumbria: wind, nuclear ...?' 'How might we understand these issues in relation to my day-to-day life?'

Avoid open-ended 'research' tasks. Rather, level the playing field by empowering pupils, including those from disadvantaged backgrounds. Set pupils up for success. Build confidence and motivation. Avoid superficial success – such as pupils copying and pasting links from Google – with no depth of learning. Enable pupils to interact deeply with challenging knowledge. Avoid busy task completion as a proxy for learning.

5. Use assessment to support learning and responsive teaching

6. Strengthen science teaching through effective professional development, as part of a monitored improvement cycle

Firstly, this will build teacher confidence and expertise around the teaching of primary science. This is key to success. This will, in turn, motivate and empower pupils.

Disadvantaged pupils don't lack talent or ability, but they can sometimes lack opportunity as a result of low family income. This is particularly true during a cost-of-living crisis that means some families are forced to think short term, managing multiple difficulties such as the costs of fuel, food and heating. Pupils who experience these challenges need the richest, highest-quality learning experiences in school.

The better we teach [disadvantaged] pupils in the classroom, the better equipped they are to build on that learning beyond the classroom and thrive in the secondary phase. They will feel motivated, included and empowered, not isolated.

Pupils with strong language, good background knowledge, self-efficacy and good self-regulation skills can thrive, even if elements of teaching, such as explanations, modelling or relationships, are not always perfect.

Pupils with more limited language, background knowledge and self-regulation skills need the highest-quality explanations, formative assessment and strong relationships. High-quality, inclusive teaching matters for all pupils, but particularly for those that find learning more difficult.

This is important, both for pupils' day-to-day experiences in the classroom and their longer-term outcomes. We need to set pupils up for long-term success as early as possible. Too often, pupils don't 'catch up later'. They need expert teaching, as early as possible, rooted in the previous five recommendations in the guidance report. But further, there is a values issue here. Disadvantaged pupils are not a problem to be solved. They are *our* pupils. Our effect size as practitioners is greatest with those pupils who may lack opportunity outside the school gates.

5. IMPACT EVALUATION

- High-quality impact evaluation is fundamental to better outcomes for disadvantaged pupils.

- Evaluation is fundamental to continuous improvement and to building a solid evidence base that will enable the plan to impact on disadvantaged pupils. It should not be treated as an optional extra. It is part of good implementation.

- Impact evaluation is about finding out whether activities and strategies have been successful, and why. It is not about proving that strategies and activities have been successful, or finding evidence to justify decision-making. It is important to decouple evaluation from accountability. Trying to prove a strategy has been successful is detrimental to improved outcomes for disadvantaged pupils. Governors should be involved in the design of the impact evaluation framework.

- When evaluating impact:
    - focus on whether activity has been successful, and in what circumstances
    - look for evidence of impact on pupil outcomes
    - put in place a robust evaluation framework at the start of the strategy
    - ensure that the evaluation framework is transparent and shared with staff and governors; it is particularly important that staff are involved in the implementation of reports on progress against that framework
    - judge any success based on outcomes for pupils not institutions
    - measure success based on outcomes for disadvantaged learners
    - ensure that intended outcomes and success criteria centre on impact on learners, rather than activities.

- When evaluating impact, avoid:
    - cherry-picking the data we are using to evaluate
    - being overly reliant on the reactions of those delivering the approach

- using vague success criteria like 'improve teaching', 'improve engagement' or 'improve reading for pleasure'
- mistaking activity – e.g. staff training – for impact.
- Case studies can be used for impact evaluation. But it is important to ensure that the pupils being used in the case studies are chosen at the start of the approach, rather than retrospectively.

The following resources can support good impact evaluation:

- the ImpactEd website: https://impacted.org.uk
- Guskey, T.R. (2002). 'Does it make a difference? Evaluating professional development', *Educational Leadership*, 59(6), pp. 45–51.
- Coe, R. (2013). 'Improving education: A triumph of hope over experience' (inaugural lecture). CEM, Durham University.
- Rowland, M. (ed.) (2021). *Addressing Educational Disadvantage in Schools and Colleges: The Essex Way*. Woodbridge: John Catt Educational ltd.

The highest form of accountability is that to our pupils and our families. Disadvantaged pupils need learning to be the best it can be. Good evaluation is key to this.

TOOLS

ASSESSMENT

How to build a holistic understanding of pupils and their needs, beyond labels

The more assessments, observations and discussions we have, the better we will understand the challenges faced by disadvantaged pupils.

Diagnostic assessment (academic and pastoral)	Pupil 1	Pupil 2	Pupil 3, etc.	Cohort
Observations of learning behaviours in the classroom				
Observations of unstructured times				
Observations of talk, listening and non-verbal communication				
Book study				
Pupil voice				
Family voice				
Teacher voice				
External expertise				
Prior attainment				
Historical trends				
Quality of teaching and learning (including recruitment and retention)				
Participation in activities (enrichment, pupil leadership)				
Others: values, attitudes, beliefs, assumptions from school staff (and the wider community)				

Key questions:

- Have we accurately assessed the needs of our pupils (academic learning, pastoral care, personal development)?
- Does the identification of need(s) provide purposeful information for leaders, teachers and support staff?
- Assessment is more than test data: see beyond test scores and chronological reading ages; consider assessments through the lens of the full curriculum and the personal development opportunities that your school offers for these pupils.

What might we mean by disadvantage?

Going beyond the label and understanding pupils as individuals is key. How does disadvantage impact learning, social inclusion and personal development?

These issues do not define pupils' educational experiences, but they can influence them. This is where we make the biggest difference. When things don't go to plan, disadvantaged pupils are impacted the most. When things go well, when we get it right, they reap the greatest benefits.

Schools are best placed to determine what disadvantage means in their own community. It might include, but is not limited to, the challenges detailed in the following table.

Challenge	Pupil 1	Pupil 2	Pupil 3, etc.	Total in cohort
Pupils eligible for the Pupil Premium				
Pupils experiencing long-term disadvantage				
Highly mobile pupils				
Pupils who are multilingual (this is a blunt label that needs deeper analysis). How do language issues impact on learning/inclusion?				
Pupils from low-income families not eligible for the Pupil Premium				
Certain ethnicities/communities that experience biases				
Pupils with long-term health conditions				

TOOLS

Challenge	Pupil 1	Pupil 2	Pupil 3, etc.	Total in cohort
Pupils whose families need additional support from external agencies				
Young carers				
Summer-born pupils				
Pupils with a close family member in prison				
Lower family education levels				
Pupils with a special educational need (again, a blunt label that needs more analysis). How does the SEND impact on learning and social inclusion?				
Pupils with low current attainment				
Pupils who are geographically isolated				
Pupils who are socially isolated				

Many pupils may experience a number of challenges that potentially impact on their learning, their wider school life and their experiences beyond the school gate. These pupils may be at greater risk of underachievement. They should be a priority for early intervention and support, and have maximum opportunities for working with high-quality, expert practitioners.

PUPIL VOICE

Understanding school life in the classroom from the perspective of pupils

These questions were designed for secondary school pupils, but could be adapted for KS1 and KS2.

Metacognition questionnaire

We want all our students to think deeply about their learning. The name we give this is metacognition. This student questionnaire, honestly answered, will help us understand our current strengths and weaknesses.

Year group

Y7   Y8   Y9   Y10   Y11

I know when I understand something.

Never   Seldom   Sometimes   Often   Always

I can make myself learn when I need to.

Never   Seldom   Sometimes   Often   Always

I try to use ways of studying that have worked for me before.

Never   Seldom   Sometimes   Often   Always

I know what the teacher expects me to learn.

Never   Seldom   Sometimes   Often   Always

I learn best when I already know something about the topic.

Never   Seldom   Sometimes   Often   Always

When I am done with my schoolwork, I ask myself if I learned what I wanted to learn.

Never   Seldom   Sometimes   Often   Always

I think of several ways to solve a problem and then choose the best one.

Never   Seldom   Sometimes   Often   Always

TOOLS

I think about what I need to learn before I start working.

Never   Seldom   Sometimes   Often   Always

I ask myself how well I am doing while I am learning something new.

Never   Seldom   Sometimes   Often   Always

I really pay attention to important information.

Never   Seldom   Sometimes   Often   Always

I learn more when I am interested in the topic.

Never   Seldom   Sometimes   Often   Always

I use my learning strengths to make up for my weaknesses.

Never   Seldom   Sometimes   Often   Always

I use different learning strategies depending on the task.

Never   Seldom   Sometimes   Often   Always

I occasionally check to make sure I'll get my work done on time.

Never   Seldom   Sometimes   Often   Always

I sometimes use learning strategies without thinking.

Never   Seldom   Sometimes   Often   Always

I ask myself if there was an easier way to do things after I finish a task.

Never   Seldom   Sometimes   Often   Always

I decide what I need to get done before I start a task.

Never   Seldom   Sometimes   Often   Always

There are subjects that I am more likely to use these strategies in.

Y/N

If you answered Y above, what subjects are they? What helps you to use these strategies?

Open text

Pupils – open questions

- Tell us about the lessons when you learn the most. When are you most successful?
- What happens in lessons when you don't learn as well?
- What do you do and what does your teacher do to help you to learn well (or not)?
- What do you have to do to be successful in your learning?
- How do you know you have been successful in your learning?
- What do you do when you get stuck/find things difficult?
- Do you think you can improve as a learner? How?
- Can you talk about some learning that you are very pleased with?
- Do you take part in the following (please provide details)?:
  - clubs
  - student leadership
  - trips and visits (curriculum based)
  - trips and visits (enrichment based)?
- Do you get any help with the following (please provide details)?:
  - resources and equipment
  - attendance
  - learning
  - wellbeing
- Further questions:
  - Do you feel like you are a valued member of the school community? Why?
  - Do you feel you are listened to?
  - Are you proud of your school?
  - What could help you to do better?
  - How often do you work with substitute teachers?
  - Does your teacher check that you understand before moving on with learning?

- What could the school do to help all children?
- Do you get good opportunities to speak/discuss/share views in class?
- Do you enjoy reading? What types of books do you enjoy?
- Is there anything you particularly dislike about school?
- Is there anything you particularly like about school?
- What are you good at?
- What would you like to improve at?
- What do you find difficult?
- What is your best memory of school (academic and social)?
- What would you like to do as a career?

STRATEGY REVIEW

Reviewing the implementation of your disadvantage strategy

Reviews are a process, not an event. They are best carried out as part of a school's own quality assurance and school improvement cycle, rather than something that is mandated. Reviews can help:

- to identify and understand how disadvantage impacts on learning
- to ascertain how well the understanding of the impact of disadvantage on learning is understood across the school
- to identify appropriate responses to the impact of disadvantage on learning
- to identify priorities
- to see how effectively those approaches and responses are being implemented and embedded
- to evaluate the impact of those responses
- to hear the voices of key stakeholders – pupils, families, staff
- to signpost to effective practice and process, research evidence and further support.

A review should include the following:

- understanding the evidence and best practice
- discussion with SLT
- discussions with pupils
- discussions with parents
- discussions with support staff
- discussions with middle leaders and teachers
- classroom observations
- intervention observations
- unstructured times
- keeping in touch and feedback
- research evidence
- reports and recommendations
- follow-up and implementation support.

Disadvantage review questions

Leadership

- Tell us about the school community, and growing up in that community as a disadvantaged pupil.
- What is the impact of socioeconomic disadvantage on pupils' learning?
- Does this vary across different phases or subject areas?

Be wary of people describing symptoms of issues, rather than the issue itself, such as progress, attendance, current attainment, chronological reading age.

Be wary of schools focusing on issues outside of their control.

- What assessments, surveys and observations have you used to identify these issues?
- How are you addressing these issues from the perspective of the following?
    - whole school
    - senior leaders
    - teachers
    - support staff
- How are you addressing these issues with regards to the following?
    - teaching and learning
    - academic intervention
    - personal development
    - pastoral care
- How well-embedded is your strategy from the perspective of the following?
    - whole school
    - senior leaders
    - teachers
    - support staff

- Is there anything that is working particularly well?
- Is there anything that isn't working so well? Why?
- Is there a collective buy-in and ownership of the issues?
- Does everyone understand their roles in addressing the impact of disadvantage?
- How are staff being developed to help them address pupil need?
- How does research evidence inform your strategy?

Be wary of a shopping list of activity. Be mindful of the need for a progression model. How are things improving? Or how are they expected to improve?

Governors
- How does disadvantage impact on pupils' learning?
- How are you addressing this?
- How well are you addressing this?
- How do you know?
- How are you evaluating the strategy and activity?

Teachers, middle leaders and support staff
- Can you describe the school's disadvantage strategy?
- How does socioeconomic disadvantage impact on learning in your class/phase/subject area?
- How is the school tackling those issues?
- How is your subject/phase addressing those issues?
- What support/professional development are you getting to address key issues?
- Look for coherence in the strategy.

Pupils
- Tell us about the lessons when you learn the most. When are you most successful?
- What happens in lessons when you don't learn as well?

- What do you do and what does your teacher do to help you to learn well (or not)?
- What do you have to do to be successful in your learning?
- How do you know you have been successful in your learning?
- What do you do when you get stuck/find things difficult?
- Can you talk about some learning that you are very pleased with?
- Further questions about enrichment, clubs, pupil leadership, personal development, attendance and more.

Parents
- How well does the school support you and your child/children?
- What's working well/less well?
- How does the school support you to help with your child's/children's learning?
- Further questions about enrichment, clubs, personal development, attendance and more.

SELF-EVALUATION TOOL

The goal of this tool is to:

- capture your initial reflections on how effective your current disadvantage strategy is
- provide a space for ongoing reflections, progress and next steps.

It is best completed as part of a team, ideally with governors and an external partner.

Three options are given for grading your school:

- **Emerging**: Limited evidence of this in your school.
- **Improving**: There is increasingly some evidence of this in your school, but it is inconsistent.
- **Mature**: There is extensive evidence of this in your school. It is embedded.

The reflection tool is based on that included in the book *Addressing Educational Disadvantage in Schools and Colleges: The Essex Way* (Rowland, 2021).

1	Expectations are high for all pupils. *Irrespective of prior attainment and FSM status, leaders, teachers and non-teaching staff are committed to the academic achievement of all pupils.*				
Building blocks		Emerging	Improving	Mature	Evidence and reflections
Leaders, teachers and non-teaching staff are ambitious for the academic attainment of all pupils, regardless of starting points and the challenges they face.					
Improving outcomes for disadvantaged pupils is a whole-school priority regardless of the proportion being low or high. There is a collective ownership of the strategy, with individuals understanding their role within it.					

TOOLS

Building blocks	Emerging	Improving	Mature	Evidence and reflections
School leaders set goals and benchmarks against the highest-performing schools rather than setting limits on what disadvantaged pupils can achieve.				
Disadvantaged pupils and their families are held in positive regard.				
Staff have a shared language around high expectations, with no use of limiting language such as 'low ability' or 'bottom set'.				
There is a good understanding of the challenges of growing up as a disadvantaged young person and the implications of this on classroom practice.				
Disadvantaged pupils do not work disproportionately with less-qualified/less-experienced staff.				
Staff discuss expectation in terms of age-related expectation, not just progress.				
Strategy and activity continually challenge and extend disadvantaged pupils.				
Disadvantaged pupils are on a trajectory to access KS5.				
Stakeholders understand and comprehend the relationship between academic achievement and self-esteem.				
Every pupil has an advocate to support them towards ambitious goals.				
All pupils have access to high-quality teaching, language and social skills.				
Disadvantage strategies prioritise pupil attainment.				
Lessons challenge pupil assumptions and enhance cultural capital.				
Classroom strategies 'scaffold up', supporting pupils to access challenging tasks, rather than 'differentiate down'.				
Where additional support in core subjects is required, this is additional and extra to the wider curriculum.				

2	Data is used to identify tightly focused improvement priorities.				
Building blocks		Emerging	Improving	Mature	Evidence and reflections
Data is a key driver for the disadvantage strategy. Assessment, not assumption, drives the strategy.					
Multiple sources of data are gathered and analysed routinely and effectively to inform strategic planning and pinpoint areas of focus. These could include diagnostic assessment (pastoral and academic), summative assessment, classroom observations, teacher voice, pupil voice and parent voice where appropriate.					
Barriers to learning identified are not just academic. There is a multi-faceted approach to ensuring pupils overcome barriers to developing the skills and experiences necessary for accessing future opportunities. However, where activity focuses on activities outside the classroom, there is a clear rationale for doing so.					
School leaders set goals and benchmarks against the highest-performing schools in their family of schools, rather than set limits on what disadvantaged pupils can achieve.					
There is a clear understanding of how socioeconomic disadvantage impacts on learning and there is a strategic plan to identify solutions. This understanding is nuanced for subject-specific and phase impact.					
Self-evaluation is rigorous and honest, drawing on a range of sources of data.					

TOOLS

3 Appropriate evidence-based teaching, academic intervention and wider approaches are used to address the root causes of underachievement.
Curriculum equity is prioritised.

Building blocks	Emerging	Improving	Mature	Evidence and reflections
A range of data is a key driver for the selection of evidence-based programmes and teaching approaches.				
Interventions are strategically selected to target key issues. They are supplementary to high-quality teaching. Low prior attainers do not get a narrower curriculum entitlement than their peers.				
Teachers and leaders are willing and able to make connections between the impact of socioeconomic disadvantage on learning and how this presents in the classroom.				
Teaching and learning staff buy into the approaches being adopted.				
All pupils, including those from disadvantaged backgrounds and low prior attainers, have equitable access to a rich, broad and balanced curriculum.				
Teachers and support staff use inclusive teaching practices to ensure all pupils can access the curriculum.				
Schools engage with and deploy research evidence on best practice for disadvantaged learners.				
School leaders are building the capacity and a collective responsibility for the implementation of the strategy.				
CPD is targeted and focused on an area of development, with pupil need in mind/targeted at the needs of disadvantaged pupils and their gaps in learning.				
CPD is compliant with the DfE's professional standards for CPD and aligned with the best evidence on effective teaching and learning.				

| 4 | School leaders train and support staff to deliver and sustain quality-first learning for all pupils, addressing pupil need in the classroom. *Professional development for teachers is prioritised.* |

Building blocks	Emerging	Improving	Mature	Evidence and reflections
The purpose of activity should be to ensure disadvantaged pupils are accessing consistently high-quality learning opportunities.				
Interventions/programmes are given a time frame and clear success criteria. They show fidelity to the evidence.				
School leaders are building the capacity of leadership teams for mentoring, coaching, planning, monitoring and evaluation.				
The highest priority for disadvantaged pupils is ensuring high-quality learning in every lesson.				
CPD is used to develop and improve inclusive teaching and learning.				
School leaders are building the capacity and a collective responsibility for the implementation of the strategy.				
CPD is targeted and focused on an area of development, with pupil need in mind/targeted at the needs of disadvantaged pupils and their gaps in learning.				
CPD is compliant with the DfE's professional standards for CPD and aligned with the best evidence on effective teaching and learning.				

5	There is a long-term, well-specified, stage-by-stage plan for addressing disadvantage.
	The plan takes into consideration the teaching and learning, academic intervention and wider approaches to support pupils.

Building blocks	Emerging	Improving	Mature	Evidence and reflections
The disadvantage strategy is based on a whole-school approach; solutions are not just a single initiative confined to isolated pockets of the school, but instead consist of a range of different strategies that reflect the complexity.				
Activities must specifically target the impact of disadvantage on learning experienced by individual students.				
Strategies target 'readiness' for next stages of life and learning to ensure that pupils access opportunities.				
The disadvantage strategy is implemented across the school in a structured and staged manner.				
Adequate time and care are taken in preparation for implementation.				
School leaders recognise that not all pupils face the same barriers and challenges.				
If funding is spent on activities outside learning, there is a clear rationale for doing so.				

6	Schools set clear outcomes for the impact of disadvantage strategies and monitor progress and quality using robust and pragmatic measures.				
	Building blocks	Emerging	Improving	Mature	Evidence and reflections
	Robust quality-assurance and impact-evaluation processes are in place to ensure success for disadvantaged learners.				
	The expected impact of a given strategy or activity is set out at the start of the implementation process.				
	A plan for robust evaluation of the disadvantage strategy is decided upon at the planning stage.				
	Schools understand the difference between monitoring and evaluation.				
	Goals for outcomes are specific, time-limited and ambitious. Those involved in the implementation of a given programme are not responsible for the evaluation.				
	Schools do not over-rely on end of year tests/GCSE results as a measurement of effectiveness of interventions (correlation/causation).				
	There is a clear process for internal quality assurance and frequent milestones.				

7	The disadvantage strategy aligns with the school's overall mission, goals and whole-school strategy. *These support a leadership environment and school climate that is conducive to changing practices across the school.*				
	Building blocks	Emerging	Improving	Mature	Evidence and reflections
	Schools have a collective, shared vision and ambition for disadvantaged pupils that recognises that academic attainment is necessary, but not sufficient, for success.				

Building blocks	Emerging	Improving	Mature	Evidence and reflections
School leadership has a clear direction and strategy for the culture and values of the school, underpinned with a plan to bring it to life.				
School leaders and teachers recognise the intersectionality between socioeconomic disadvantage and other areas of vulnerability.				
The whole school community is engaged with the school's mission on disadvantage.				
Disadvantaged pupils feel included in the school community, in lessons and in wider school life.				
The disadvantage strategy dovetails clearly with/is at the heart of the overarching school development plan: there is a clear sense of how Pupil-Premium-funded activity works towards achieving the school's overarching improvement aims.				
Disadvantage is an important item in leadership meetings, staff meetings, subject meetings and phase meetings.				
There is a trajectory of improved attainment for disadvantaged pupils.				
Middle leaders/leadership-implementation teams are critical in ensuring that strategies are actioned in the classroom consistently (they are critical for internal QA).				
The disadvantage strategy is integrated into senior- and middle-leadership roles.				
Leaders and teachers are consistent in upholding the school culture and they embody the culture and values of the school as models to the pupils.				

8	Outcome of reflection process
Emerging strengths	
Next steps for school leaders	

TOOLS

PUPIL TRACKING

Tracking disadvantaged/lower-attaining pupils – looking at their lived experience through the school day or week – can provide invaluable insights, from their perspective. How does this compare to their peers and their experiences of school life?

This exercise will be enhanced if the pupils in the disadvantaged group and the non-disadvantaged group can be randomly selected.

Are they working with high-quality teachers and support staff?
- During observations, are pupils working with experienced teachers?
- Are pupils working with subject specialists?
- Are any interventions led by effectively trained staff?

Observation	Pupil A	Pupil B	Pupil C	Pupil D	Pupil E	Pupil F

Observation	Pupil G	Pupil H	Pupil I	Pupil J	Pupil K	Pupil L

How often are they working with unqualified staff or supply staff?
- Are pupils working with TAs? Inside the classroom or outside?
- Are pupils working with cover or supply teachers?
- Are pupils attending school?

Observation	Pupil A	Pupil B	Pupil C	Pupil D	Pupil E	Pupil F

Observation	Pupil G	Pupil H	Pupil I	Pupil J	Pupil K	Pupil L

Do they get meaningful opportunities to interact with their peers?

- During collaborative learning, are pupils working with their peers or adults?
- Is there individual accountability during group tasks?
- Are pupils actively participating? Are they sat alone?

Observation	Pupil A	Pupil B	Pupil C	Pupil D	Pupil E	Pupil F

Observation	Pupil G	Pupil H	Pupil I	Pupil J	Pupil K	Pupil L

Do they get thinking time before engaging in questioning and discussion?

- Do pupils get time before engaging in 'think – pair – share'?
- Are pupils given time and space before answering, especially during cold calling?
- Are pupils able to opt out of questioning, reading aloud or similar?

Observation	Pupil A	Pupil B	Pupil C	Pupil D	Pupil E	Pupil F

Observation	Pupil G	Pupil H	Pupil I	Pupil J	Pupil K	Pupil L

What types of feedback do they get on their learning and their learning behaviours?

- Is feedback encouraging? Is it metacognitive?
- Are there consistent expectations/are pupils able to opt out?
- Do pupils have their books/necessary resources with them?

Observation	Pupil A	Pupil B	Pupil C	Pupil D	Pupil E	Pupil F

Observation	Pupil G	Pupil H	Pupil I	Pupil J	Pupil K	Pupil L

How often are they late/out of lessons during learning time?

- Are pupils punctual?
- Are pupils in lessons?
- Are they adhering to behaviour expectations?

Observation	Pupil A	Pupil B	Pupil C	Pupil D	Pupil E	Pupil F

Observation	Pupil G	Pupil H	Pupil I	Pupil J	Pupil K	Pupil L

What is their experience during lunch and break?

- Are pupils positively interacting with peers?
- Do they eat lunch with other pupils?
- Are they engaging in available activities (games, clubs, drop-ins)?

Observation	Pupil A	Pupil B	Pupil C	Pupil D	Pupil E	Pupil F

Observation	Pupil G	Pupil H	Pupil I	Pupil J	Pupil K	Pupil L

What additional activities are they involved in?

- Are pupils involved in student leadership?
- Are pupils involved in clubs/enrichment?
- Are pupils representing houses/school in sport/performing arts etc.?

Observation	Pupil A	Pupil B	Pupil C	Pupil D	Pupil E	Pupil F

Observation	Pupil G	Pupil H	Pupil I	Pupil J	Pupil K	Pupil L

How often are they in isolation/in detention/suspended?

- Have pupils been sanctioned for behaviour issues in the last year?
- Have pupils been in detention in the last year?
- Have pupils been suspended in the last year?

Observation	Pupil A	Pupil B	Pupil C	Pupil D	Pupil E	Pupil F

Observation	Pupil G	Pupil H	Pupil I	Pupil J	Pupil K	Pupil L

Pupil voice

Discuss:

'Me and my friends do well at school.'

'What do you do when you find learning difficult?'

'What helps you to improve as a learner?'

'Does feedback help you improve? How?'

'Do you make a positive contribution to the school?'

'How would you improve your school experiences (in class and out)?'

ACKNOWLEDGEMENTS

Thank you so much to everyone that contributed to this book, formally and informally.

Jon Eaton
Rowena Lucas
Shaun Allison
Cathy Potter
Tiffnie Harris
Thomas McMorrin
Phil Stock
Matt Williams
Rupinder Bansil
Luke Welsh
Michelle Henley
Timi Alabi
Anna Bewsher
Stella Jones
Jamie Whiteside
C.J. Rauch
Neil Stirrat
Lisa Wise
Marianne Enchill-Balogun
Tim Coulson
Patty Williams
Dan Nicholls
Kate Cliffe
Andy Samways
Ness Bally
Sophie Chaloner
Andrew Willis
Lyn Wright

Philippa Holliday
Christine Gilbert
George Lumley
Chris Runeckles
Katie Evans
Louise Sim
Ellice Camfield-Grant
John Rodgers
Ian Tankard
Kay Turner
Susie Fraser
Sarah Green
Kate Wilkins
John Casson
Roz Burch
Naureen Kausar
Amanda Jennings
Yvette Thomas
David Bartram
Margaret Mulholland
Roy Blatchford
Fiona Fearon
Scott Fletcher
Toni Hazen
Michele Miller
Kate Frood
Sean O'Regan

And everyone else that I have chatted to about this issue! A final thank you to Brett Court and Lydia Kelly for all their help.

REFERENCES

Beck, I.L., McKeown, M.G. & Kucan, L. (2013). *Bringing Words to Life: Robust vocabulary instruction*. New York: The Guilford Press.

Blatchford, P. & Russell, A. (2020). *Rethinking Class Size: The complex story of impact on teaching and learning*. London: UCL Press.

British Psychological Society (2017). 'Behaviour change: School attendance, exclusion and persistent absence'. Available at: https://cms.bps.org.uk/sites/default/files/2022-07/Behaviour%20Change%20-%20School%20attendance%2C%20exclusion%20and%20persistent%20absence%20%282017%29.pdf

Coe, R. (2013) 'Improving education: A triumph of hope over experience' (inaugural lecture). CEM, Durham University

Crenna-Jennings, W. (2018). 'Key drivers of the disadvantage gap: Literature review'. Education in England: Annual report 2018. Education Policy Institute. Available at: https://epi.org.uk/wp-content/uploads/2018/07/EPI-Annual-Report-2018-Lit-review.pdf

Department for Education (DfE) (2020). 'Mathematics guidance: key stages 1 and 2'. Available at: https://assets.publishing.service.gov.uk/media/6140b7008fa8f503ba3dc8d1/Maths_guidance_KS_1_and_2.pdf

Department for Education (DfE) (2024). 'Pupil premium: Overview (Guidance)'. Available at: www.gov.uk/government/publications/pupil-premium/pupil-premium

Education Endowment Foundation (EEF) Teaching and Learning Toolkit. Available at: https://educationendowmentfoundation.org.uk/education-evidence/teaching-learning-toolkit

Education Endowment Foundation (EEF) (2021a). 'Working with parents to support children's learning'. Available at: https://educationendowmentfoundation.org.uk/education-evidence/guidance-reports/supporting-parents

Education Endowment Foundation (EEF) (2021b). 'Improving mathematics in the Early Years and Key Stage 1'. Available at: https://educationendowmentfoundation.org.uk/education-evidence/guidance-reports/early-maths

Education Endowment Foundation (EEF) (2023). 'Improving primary science'. Available at: https://educationendowmentfoundation.org.uk/education-evidence/guidance-reports/primary-science-ks1-ks2

Education Endowment Foundation (EEF) (2024a). 'A school's guide to implementation'. Available at: https://educationendowmentfoundation.org.uk/education-evidence/guidance-reports/implementation

Education Endowment Foundation (EEF) (2024b). 'The EEF guide to the Pupil Premium'. Available at: https://educationendowmentfoundation.org.uk/education-evidence/using-pupil-premium

Education Endowment Foundation (EEF) (2024c). 'Using research evidence: A concise guide'. Available at: https://educationendowmentfoundation.org.uk/education-evidence/more-resources-and-support/using-research-evidence

Education Policy Institute (2024). Annual report, 2024. Available at: https://epi.org.uk/publications-and-research/annual-report-2024/

Ellis, S. & Tod, J. (2018). *Behaviour for Learning: Promoting positive relationships in the classroom*. London: Routledge.

Feely, M. & Karlin, B. (2023). *The Teaching and Learning Playbook: Examples of excellence in teaching*. London: Routledge.

Gorard, S. (2023). 'Poorer pupils do worse at school – here's how to reduce the attainment gap'. Available at: https://theconversation.com/poorer-pupils-do-worse-at-school-heres-how-to-reduce-the-attainment-gap-205535

Guskey, T.R. (2002). 'Does it make a difference? Evaluating professional development', *Educational Leadership*, 59(6), pp. 45–51.

Harris, M. (2018). 'I have forgotten how to read'. *The Globe and Mail*.

Holub, M. (2006). 'A Boy's Head', in *Poems Before and After*. Hexham, Northumberland: Bloodaxe Books.

Joseph Rowntree Foundation (2016). 'Special educational needs and their links to poverty'. Available at: www.jrf.org.uk/child-poverty/special-educational-needs-and-their-links-to-poverty

Joseph Rowntree Foundation (2023). '5.7 million low-income households having to cut down or skip meals, as JRF's cost of living tracker shows "Horrendous new normal"'. Available at: https://www.jrf.org.uk/news/57-million-low-income-households-having-to-cut-down-or-skip-meals-as-jrfs-cost-of-living

Joseph Rowntree Foundation (2024). 'Public services staggering under the weight of hardship as politicians urged to fix it "at source"'. Available at: https://www.jrf.org.uk/news/public-services-staggering-under-the-weight-of-hardship

Kahneman, D. (2011). *Thinking, Fast and Slow*. New York: Penguin.

McCrory Calarco, J. (2014). 'Coached for the Classroom: Parents' Cultural Transmission and Children's Reproduction of Educational Inequalities', *American Sociological Review*, 79(5). doi: 10.1177/0003122414546931

OneCornwall (2024). 'Transforming attendance in Cornwall'. Available at: www.onecornwall.co.uk/_site/data/publications/attendance_booklet/index.html

Osher, D., Cantor, P., Berg, J., Steyer, L. & Rose, T. (2020). 'Drivers of human development: How relationships and context shape learning and development', *Applied Developmental Science*, 24(1), pp.6–36.

Resolution Foundation (2023). The Living Standards Outlook 2023. https://www.resolutionfoundation.org/app/uploads/2023/01/Living-Standards-Outlook-2023.pdf?utm_source=chatgpt.com

Rosenshine, B. (2012). 'Principles of instruction'. *American Educator*. Available at: www.teachertoolkit.co.uk/wp-content/uploads/2018/10/Principles-of-Insruction-Rosenshine.pdf

Rowland, M. (ed.). (2021). *Addressing Educational Disadvantage in Schools and Colleges: The Essex Way*. Woodbridge: John Catt Educational Ltd.

Royal Holloway University of London (2023). 'Improving reading skills helps transition to secondary school'. Available at: www.royalholloway.ac.uk/about-us/news/improving-reading-skills-helps-transition-to-secondary-school/

TES (2024). 'Half of students 'disadvantaged' on work experience'. Available at: www.tes.com/magazine/news/secondary/half-state-school-students-disadvantaged-by-lack-of-work-experience-university-access

The Sutton Trust (2022). 'Speaking up'. Available at: www.suttontrust.com/our-research/speaking-up-accents-social-mobility/

Tierney, S. (2017). 'Absences matter and you can help'. Available at: https://leadinglearner.me/2017/07/02/absences-matter-and-you-can-help/

UCL (2017). 'Reading improves teenagers' vocab, whatever their background, say researchers'. Centre for Longitudinal Studies, UCL. Available at: https://cls.ucl.ac.uk/reading-improves-teenagers-vocab-whatever-their-background-say-researchers/

University of Missouri (2017). 'Students more likely to succeed if teachers have positive perceptions of parents'. Available at: https://munewsarchives.missouri.edu/news-releases/2017/0220-students-more-likely-to-succeed-if-teachers-have-positive-perceptions-of-parents/

Waldfogel, J. & Washbrook, E. (2010). 'Low income and early cognitive development in the UK'. The Sutton Trust. Available at: https://www.suttontrust.com/our-research/low-income-early-cognitive-development-u-k/

The A–Z series focuses on the 'fun and fundamentals' of what's happening in primary, special and secondary schools today. Each title is written by a leading practitioner, adopting a series approach of reflection, advice and provocation.

As a group of authors with a strong belief in the power of education to shape and change young people's lives, we hope teachers and leaders in the UK and internationally enjoy what we have to say.

Roy Blatchford, series editor

The A–Z of Great Classrooms (2023)

The A–Z of Secondary Leadership (2023)

The A–Z of Primary Maths (2024)

The A–Z of School Improvement (2024)

The A–Z of Diversity and Inclusion (2024)

The A–Z of Trust Leadership (2024)

The A–Z of International School Leadership (2024)

The A–Z of Special Educational Needs (2024)

The A–Z of Early Career Teaching (2024)

The A–Z of Student Wellbeing (2025)

The A–Z of Addressing Disadvantage (2025)

The A–Z of Good Governance (forthcoming)

The A–Z of Primary Leadership (forthcoming)

The A–Z of Independent School Leadership (forthcoming)

The A–Z of Primary English (forthcoming)